THE
BEST OF
CANADA
Cookbook

THE BEST OF CANADA Cookbook

Tony Roldan & Jim White

McClelland and Stewart

The Canadian Publishers
McClelland and Stewart Limited
25 Hollinger Road, Toronto M4B 3G2

Canadian Cataloguing in Publication Data
Roldan, Tony, 1924-
   The best of Canada cookbook
Includes index.
ISBN 0-7710-7714-9

1. Cookery, Canadian.   I. White, Jim 1946-
II. Title.

TX715.R64   641.5971   C81-094698-X

Manufactured in Canada by Webcom Limited

To Margarith, for the patience she displayed
while I made a mess in her kitchen

T.R.

To Anne and Bill, who first introduced me to
Tony's sole,
and to Carol, who nourishes me with hers today

J.W.

ACKNOWLEDGEMENTS

Behind every good chef is a team, behind every good writer is an editor, and behind every good man there is always a woman. We are fortunate to have had the support and encouragement of numerous individuals in the preparation of our book. Foremost, we thank our wives (one each!): Margarith, who performed the work of a kitchen brigade in chopping, chilling, and chipping in, and Carol, who guided me, nay nudged me, through canyons of cookbook editing. We also want to thank our editor, Jennifer Glossop, for her crayony clean-up of a manuscript stained with sauces and tasty oils. Thanks to Sara Jane Kennerley for her indexing, and to Ian Somerville at the *Toronto Star* for his initial input in the design of our book.

Personally, I want to thank my two wonderful children, Jennifer and Jason, who exhibited hours of adult patience in delayed meals and postponed family activities while I displayed, all too often, the temperamental tantrums of a child during our frenzied cooking-writing-editing periods.

Thanks to Shelley Kanter for her moral support, and finally, our gratitude to Marty Kovnats, friend and professional who proved that behind every team of good authors there is a good lawyer.

Jim White
Tony Roldan

CONTENTS

INTRODUCTION

The memory is fuzzy, faded, and old. Yet it is sweet and has a pleasant softness around the edges. It's from many years back, maybe 1961 or 1962. Thanksgiving. My dad and I are in the car, heading into a rainstorm that has the fury of a food processor stuck on high. The trees are bowed by the wind, resembling catapults ready to sling their few remaining leaves.

We are driving south on Toronto's Yonge Street. Ours is a rendezvous with dinner as well as, it turns out, with destiny. It is an experiment, bold and delicious. If it works once, it will work again and again.

We turn off Yonge into an alley, a back lane. We pile out; the pelting rain stings. We knock furiously at a black back door; inside there is the sound of commotion, of bustle. When the door swings open, aromas escape like steam from a soufflé. There are smells of warm baked bread, of cinnamony apple pie, the buttery bouquet of roasted turkey.

This is the kitchen of the Westbury Hotel, where we have come to pick up a 25-pound turkey, personally roasted for us by sous-chef (in those days) Tony Roldan. Our aim is to race home before friends and family arrive and set a festive spread. There isn't a tastier, better stuffed bird than Tony's (so my father and mother used to tell me and I now believe).

That was the first time I met Tony, or visited his hot, steamy kitchen. But it would not be the last. I'd heard so much about Tony's stovemanship I expected a fairy-tale-tall figure to tower over me (remember: I was a kid). But here he was, this chef, no taller than me, a friendly man with a smile as warm as a freshly baked loaf of bread. We talked briefly, took the golden roasted turkey and arrived home before the company.

Everyone commented on what a wonderful bird my family had prepared. Tender, succulent, juicy. And the stuffing. Mmmmmm. We didn't explain anything; just sat there with our mouths closed. (But then it's impolite to talk with your mouth full. . . .)

This family scene replayed itself many Thanksgivings – without any misgivings – until I went off to Africa and Tony went off to another hotel.

An unusual beginning for a cookbook, perhaps, but no less unusual a beginning for a friendship with Tony that has spanned 20 years.

Tony's gone on to become one of Canada's great chefs, captain of our team to the 1976 World Culinary Olympics in Frankfurt, West Germany, where Canada placed second in world cooking competition; he's an innovative cook, an experimental farmer of sorts, a chef dedicated to cooking the best of Canada.

Me, I've gone on to become a professional photographer, a journalist, broadcaster, and a TV and radio producer. I lived in Africa for several years, and now, I'm the food writer-editor and restaurant critic for the *Toronto Star*. A meandering career shaped by food.

I've made films and filmstrips with food themes in Kenya, Lesotho, Algeria, as well as in Malaysia and Indonesia; have travelled the Sahel (sub-Saharan North Africa) to record famine – the lack of food. And as one needs a strong stomach to travel through war zones as I have done in Africa, so, too, one needs a large stomach to be a full-time food writer-editor – one dedicated to defining and discovering the best of Canada.

It was destined, I guess, that Tony and I would join forces to cook and write *The Best of Canada*. As it happens, our lives have been woven like the lattice top on an apple pie. My parents were crazy for Tony's cooking and dined at least once every week for 12 years at the Westbury. While I wasn't always with them, it's obvious that my tastebuds were being shaped secondhand through homecooking that must have resembled the chef's.

Every family birthday from 1963 and many, many Sunday brunches were spent at the Westbury. I didn't realize it until our recipe development was completed and I was here – pounding away at the keys – but Tony even cooked the extraordinary dinner I had at the Westbury in July 1972 to celebrate my engagement. Every time I turn around, there's Tony Roldan – dressed in his whites, playing with his sauces.

*   *   *

"Saucy." That's what Tony's mother used to call him. Not so much because he was a saucy kid (which he probably was, due to his Spanish temper!), but because he loved to futz around in the kitchen, to make sauces as much as a mess.

Tony says he wanted to become a doctor but fate intervened. The Spanish-born chef has a *curriculum vitae* that reads like Candide's. Because of the Civil War in Spain in 1938 and his father's position in the civil guard, Tony *et famille* were forced to flee. The 14-year-old lad was separated from his parents and adopted as a refugee by a French family that operated an inn near St. Emilion.

It was here that Tony learned to cook and make wine. He worked in the country kitchen until Europe's war spilled over into France; then he was forced to hide and work in the Pyrenees. But only for three months; the Germans captured our roving, unpassported chef and deported him to a submarine base in the Loire Valley where he was forced to work at hard labour until 1944.

Tony escaped and returned to Spain. He was recaptured – this time by the Spanish – and accused of political crimes. Tony escaped a second time, back across the Pyrenees into France. Again, with Voltairean swiftness, the plot shifts; somehow, some way, in a manner far too convoluted to describe in a cookbook, Tony *et famille* were reunited in England where the chef landed work as a saucier and cook in some of the finest hotels in London. Ten years later, in 1957, Tony took the plunge – or is it lunge? – and came to Canada to eke out his fortunes and, coincidentally, to meet me.

It sounds intriguing as the plot of a paperback thriller. There is, Tony concludes, only one thing as epic – the year we've just spent cooking and creating dishes for *The Best of Canada*. By day, Tony's been a corporate chef for a chain of hotels (Sutton Place and Bristol Place), by night and weekend, an inventor of dishes for this book. Likewise, I've been a food editor by day, a restaurant critic by night, and an experimental cook and notetaker on weekends. Broken plates there were many; broken dreams there were none.

What we've attempted to do is cook Canadian. To us, Canadian cuisine is cooking with what's around, using what's fresh and seasonally available. Canadian cuisine, of necessity, relies on long-established European (and some Oriental) cooking techniques. But our combinations are original. More than half the recipes in this volume were created especially for *The Best of Canada*.

*   *   *

Until now, curious outsiders and national gastronomes have tried to define Canadian cuisine – *la cuisine canadienne* – in historic and geographic terms. It works and it doesn't work but, for the most part, culinary theory misses the mark: it hasn't got much taste.

Some say authentic Canadian cooking is frontier food. Historically, we owe a great deal to our native peoples, the first inhabitants of the continent, for their food gifts. Our Indian brethren introduced us to corn, potatoes, peanuts, pumpkins, and pecans. You couldn't sit down to a good old-fashioned strawberry sundae with nuts today if it weren't for our Indian forefathers. But this is hardly Canadian cuisine, or is it?

Some peg truly Canadian cuisine to the arrival of the French. Many citizens today name dishes such as tourtière, Québec's meat pie, or French Canadian split-pea soup as being identifiably Canadian. But this is hardly the apex of Canadian cuisine, or is it?

The immigrant waves that have hit our shores these last 250 years have been more like tidal waves, at least gastronomically. The English and Scots brought their breads, the Germans (sometimes mistakenly called Dutch because of a mistranslation of Deutsch) brought schmier-kase and shoo-fly pie; similarly, our tastes and our waistlines have been shaped by the gastrocultural activities of Hungarian, Chinese, Italian, Ukrainian, Greek, Finnish, Estonian, Japanese, Middle Eastern, and Scandinavian settlers.

Our table spreads are now so diverse that even choosing breakfast, never mind lunch and dinner, has become a problem: will it be Chinese dim sum, German pancakes, Jewish bagels, Scandinavian smorgasbord, or French croissants with a glass of O.J.?

Historically, Canadian cuisine is the sum of what all our diverse ethno-cultural groups brought with them in the way of food. A dinner tonight in Chinatown hardly seems an example of Canadian cuisine, though it's a part.

Most of our professional chefs today are trained to duplicate the cooking of Europe: classical French, modish Mediterranean, intriguing Italian. Europe, however, has a 500-year head start on cooking, on seasoning, on appreciating food. To try blindly to duplicate the best cooking of Europe is not, of itself, a method to produce the best of Canada.

European cooking has evolved over centuries, itself the amalgam of diverse cultural groups. Canada, by contrast, is a young nation, a mere 114 years old; I have tasted some of Europe's finest wines – her Tokays and Bordeaux – that are older than Canada. We must not rush things. Moreover, Tony and I believe that *cuisine canadienne* must not rely rigidly on classical European cooking techniques that are based on Europe's own regional foods – the game, fruits, and vegetables that do not grow here.

Geographically, gastronomes insist that for something to be truly Canadian, it must originate here. Given this definition, *cuisine canadienne* has an appealing, colourful, but terribly limited, dimension.

McIntosh apples are red and identifiably Ontarian, fiddleheads are green and oh-so New Brunswickian, wild rice is Manitoba's strong suit, Malpeque oysters belong to the Maritimes, Arctic char, Winnipeg goldeye and B.C. salmon come from our abundant waters (quickly becoming less abundant, one must add). But surely, to define a cuisine by only what is native to one's soils is gastronomically short-sighted. There must be some allowance in defining a national cuisine for social, cultural, and political inputs.

If not, the Japanese would never have been able to claim tempura as their own. After all, it was the Portuguese who carried the Italian technique of deep-frying to the East where it was fine-tuned to local taste.

Hoping to broaden the sphere of what grows in Canada, Tony has trial plots of many exotic vegetables at his home-cum-farm in King City, north of Toronto. Canadians may soon be enjoying his cardoon, mâche, kohlrabi, or sorrel, and they'll be re-introduced to a vegetable he's growing that was, in origin, indigenous to this continent–Jerusalem artichokes.

As some of these "new" foods will appear in Canadian supermarkets with increasing frequency in years ahead, we've included recipes utilizing them.

*   *   *

As much as we hope to introduce Canadians to a new style of cuisine–using combinations of foods that grow in abundance here–we also hope to steer them away from *cuisine styrene*–a bland diet of packaged foods and dull tasting, out-of-season produce.

Something has happened to the tastebuds of *Homo urbanis* who is so accepting of *cuisine styrene* that he thinks cheese must come wrapped in individual plastic sleeves to be cheese. My kids bring this kind of viewpoint home from school. If this were the case, however, man would have been given incinerators, not intestines, to dispose of the stuff.

Tony and I believe that to cook properly you must use the freshest seasonal produce; uniformity may be something desirable in tennis balls but not tomatoes. A *real* tomato, grown in *real* soil, picked at the height of summer ripeness is one thing, but the tennis-ball-textured tomatoes that are picked green, gassed, and shipped from the south throughout winter, have no more taste than they do texture.

Our dishes have one outstanding, common characteristic: they taste wonderful. Each recipe relies on each season's freshest and best-tasting produce. There is only one time of year to make our Cold Terrine of Summer Vegetables served with a dill sauce: at the height of summer.

Before you set out for market, or when you return, check our index to determine what is the best dish you might create using the fruits, vegetables, and meats just at their peak.

Our basic tenet is: don't overseason. Which means *don't cook certain dishes once the season's over.* It also means don't kill the natural taste of ingredients with megaspoons of spice. Cooks must respect the natural taste and texture of foods; meals shouldn't be swimming in sharp sauces. The flavour of food should be enhanced, not obliterated, by seasoning.

14

Chefs are like artists in many ways; they give great thought to their palates (palettes) and colour is a primary concern. At the height of summer, our Red Pepper and Blueberry Salad is a delicious work of contrast. It isn't meant to be tackled in February when you should be brushstroking your palate with our divine Hubbard Squash Bisque, an original soup for *The Best of Canada.*

Without being extravagant of cost, we have tried to be inventive of spirit; good cooking is limited only by the imagination of the chef. Here, then, you'll find:

• an omelette made without eggs (Yam and Apple Omelette)

• a dessert made with Canada's very own springtime sweetener – a maple syrup mousse

• a delicious, colorful and *new* garnish – Yam and Chive Salad

• a 7-day meal plan to feed a family of four for an entire week with *one* turkey and *never have a single dinner of leftovers!*

Ingredients for Cooking

FRESH

Nothing tastes fresher than fresh, but nothing tastes worse than a fresh vegetable out of season. We don't have many canned foods in our home, but a can of tomatoes beats anything fresh you can buy in the middle of winter.

Consequently, we have modified some recipes to be used year-round; frozen and canned foods do have supporting roles in the kitchen cast and should not be denied the occasional spotlight.

WINES

If you won't drink it, sink it. Don't ever cook with a wine that you wouldn't consider drinking; there's only one place for such vinegared vino: down the drain.

Many of our recipes call for wine that will be reduced for a sauce; reduction only heightens the essence of a wine, concentrates the grape. Better to open a *new, good* wine, use half a cup for a recipe and then drink the rest with the meal, than to use half a cup of 2-week-old refrigerated "cooking wine" that may actually ruin your recipe.

BUTTER

We prefer to cook with unsalted butter. There's a lot of myth about why good cooks use it. Some chefs argue that it doesn't burn as easily as salted butter. A check with specialists with a degree in BS (Butter Science) confirms, however, that this isn't so. While sodium chloride (the salt in butter) is a good conductor of heat, you'd not only be out on a limb-but sawing it off-to suggest that it makes butter burn more quickly.

No, the reason good cooks prefer using unsalted butter (sometimes called "sweet" butter) is for *taste*. Unsalted butter just tastes better and doesn't have a certain "soapy" quality that salted butter sometimes gets when heated.

PEPPER

Whenever a recipe calls for coarsely ground or crushed pepper, we recommend crushing whole peppercorns with a heavy skillet, in a mortar with pestle, or with a pepper mill. Coarsely ground pepper has a taste *very* different from that of finely milled, almost dust-like pepper. There is no substitute, as far as we're concerned, in a recipe calling for *coarsely* ground (or crushed) pepper.

And while on the subject, there's also no substitute for "*freshly* ground pepper," which is what many recipes require. Freshly ground pepper comes out of a pepper mill as *you* grind it; it bears no relation to that flavourless dust found in pepper "shakers" that, for all you know, may have been ground just after Confederation. Or could have served as confetti at that occasion.

SAUCE REDUCTIONS

Many of our meat dishes require reducing a sauce "until thick enough to coat a wooden spoon." The Italians have an expression that is much more colourful: "reduce sauce until it sheds one tear." Another way of saying reduce the sauce to the point where one sad, lonely drop, or tear, falls from the spoon when it is lifted from the sauce.

Most sauces in our book are finished-unless otherwise noted-when your spoon sheds a tear.

Terms in This Book

SAUTÉ PAN

Frequent use is made of this term in our recipes, although a frying pan or skillet will serve the home cook equally well. A sauté pan is a wide heavy-bottomed pan with fairly high, straight sides; French and professional cooks prefer this utensil for making sauces because ingredients have a tendency to jump as the pan is shaken back and forth across the burner.

Sauter, wouldn't you know it, is the French verb "to jump." Today, many cooks use the verbs – as well as the pans – *to fry* and *to sauté* interchangeably, although pros insist there's a difference. To sauté means to cook something in a very small amount of butter, oil, lard, or fat, one side at a time. To fry implies that a more generous quantity of cooking fat is used, and if you're too generous, you'll have moved up the scale to deep-frying.

A good sauté pan is made of copper lined with tin, aluminum, or stainless steel; it should transmit heat evenly and quickly. It should have a long handle, preferably joined to the pan, not an extension of it. A lid is useful.

PREHEATED BROILER

Occasionally, reference is made to placing food beneath a preheated broiler; much as you preheat your oven to bake certain dishes properly, so, too, is preheating an electric broiler necessary for some recipes.

With a hot, hot broiler you immediately sear meats, sealing in juices that might otherwise ooze out as the broiling element slowly reaches its peak; if your vegetables have a dusting of grated cheese that you want to set golden, you require a hot broiler to melt the cheese, not a getting-warmer-and-warmer element that half stews the vegetables underneath the crust of cheese.

POWDERED CHICKEN STOCK

This ingredient is sold variously as chicken broth mix, powdered chicken broth, and chicken soup base. What we have in mind is the powdered stuff that you add to water to make instant chicken stock.

Many cooks prefer chicken bouillon cubes, and we have no objection to their use. However, not all our recipes require dissolving the instant chicken. For this reason we've standardized the term: powdered chicken stock. Although nothing, obviously, beats a made-from-scratch version of the real thing.

METRICS
We believe that cooking in metric is actually quite simple. For those who have taken the kilopascal plunge or who have dabbled their digits in decilitres, we present the system endorsed by the Canadian Home Economics Association.

ESSENTIAL NON-ESSENTIALS
Many cookbooks require that before you even tackle one recipe you make half a dozen sauces, stocks, and dressings to be used throughout the book as a basis for many dishes. We have tried to avoid this; nearly all recipes stand on their own. The few that require specialty ingredients were included because there are limited available commercial substitutes. For example, a few recipes call for crystallized ginger. You will find this ingredient in many Chinese grocery stores and many urban supermarkets. You can make your own, however, quite easily and inexpensively, and so we've included a recipe (page 222).

Likewise, crème fraîche. This is France's slightly soured clotted cream; because it is not sweet it complements many desserts and pies better than whipped cream. Gourmet shops and some supermarkets now sell imported crème fraîche, but since nothing can match the taste of homemade, we've included a recipe. All it takes is heavy cream and buttermilk.

During the year that we developed and tested our recipes, we became aware that there is only one thing equal in importance to having a good meal: having a good appetite. In fact, as you thumb through and try our recipes, we think you'll recognize that this is as much a culinary work as a work of love; for this reason, it is as much a celebration of the heart as it is the stomach.

Happy cooking.

Happy eating.

Jim White

MENUS FOR EVERY SEASON

SUMMER

COLD

Cold Terrine of Summer Vegetables with Dill Sauce
(page 34)

* * *

Chilled Fillets of Rainbow Trout with Dill Sauce
(page 78)

* * *

Soft-Boiled Egg in Aspic with Nova Scotia Salmon
(page 29)

* * *

Red Pepper and Blueberry Salad
(page 167)

HOT

Yam and Apple Omelette
(page 160)

* * *

Best-Ever Quiche Lorraine
(page 41)

* * *

Braised Beef with Herbs and Hazelnuts
(page 83)

* * *

Blueberry River Blueberry Bread
(page 190)

DESSERT

Rocky Mountain Raspberry Cake
(page 200)

* * *

Niagara Falls Trifle
(page 208)

FALL

HOMESTYLE

Hubbard Squash Bisque
(page 59)

* * *

Roast Ontario Pork Stuffed with Ginger and Coconut
(page 106)

* * *

Best-Ever Broccoli
(page 142)

* * *

Persimmon Chiffon Pie
(page 204)

ELEGANT ENTERTAINING

Artichokes Vinaigrette
(page 30)

* * *

Scampi in Love
(page 72)

* * *

Lemon and Parsley Rice
(page 185)

* * *

Sunday Grilled Spring Chicken
(page 120)

* * *

Kohlrabi with Béchamel Sauce
(page 146)

* * *

Tender Romaine Lettuce with Tarragon Salad Dressing
(page 166)

* * *

Peach Champagne Sabayon
(page 210)

Settlers' Soup
(page 58)

* * *

Cordon Blue Turkey Breast Stuffed with Spinach and
Emmenthal Cheese
(page 132)

* * *

Potato and Turnip Casserole
(page 149)

* * *

Beet and Apple Salad
(page 176)

* * *

Favourite Canadian Apple Pie
(page 205)

OR

Boneless Stuffed Turkey Leg
(page 131)

* * *

Bradford Brussel Sprouts
(page 144)

* * *

Gingered Carrots
(page 155)

* * *

Celery Root Salad with Yogurt and Tarragon
(page 171)

* * *

Northern Spy Apple Cake
(page 192)

WINTER

HOMESTYLE

Budget Bean and Turnip Soup
(page 50)

* * *

1929 Hamburger
(page 87)

* * *

Julia's Potato Waffles
(page 148)

* * *

Northern Spy Apple Cake
(page 192)

ELEGANT ENTERTAINING

Tomato and Tarragon Soup
(page 55)

* * *

Atlantic Seafood Trawler: Saffron Scallops and Shrimp
(page 71)

* * *

Royale de Canard Canadien
(page 114)

* * *

Fennel with Lemon and Cheese
(page 160)

* * *

Broccoli Purée
(page 142)

* * *

TNT Salad
(page 177)

* * *

Maple Leaf Mousse
(page 202)

COLD

Perfect *Pâté Maison*
(page 36)

* * *

Elegant Canadian Crab Meat Salad
(page 170)

* * *

Easy Eggplant Salad
(page 173)

HOT

Grand Bank Lobster Crêpes
(page 66)

* * *

Selkirk Spinach Quiche
(page 40)

* * *

Potato Omelette
(page 43)

* * *

Chicken Rosemary
(page 116)

* * *

Whole-Wheat Health Bread
(page 191)

DESSERT

Margarith's Hazelnut Coffee Ring
(page 194)

* * *

Sutton Place Amaretto Cheesecake
(page 193)

SPRING

Hard-Boiled Eggs Stuffed with Smoked Salmon Mousse
(page 28)

* * *

Perfect *Pâté Maison*
(page 36)

* * *

Simple Pickled Mushrooms
(page 33)

* * *

Zucchini Fritters
(page 162)

* * *

Potato Omelette
(page 43)

* * *

Green Pepper and Egg Sandwich Spread
(page 42)

* * *

Cream of Smoked Salmon Ladyfinger Sandwiches
(page 31)

* * *

Sutton Place Amaretto Cheesecake
(page 193)

* * *

Margarith's Hazelnut Coffee Ring
(page 194)

APPETIZERS

HARD-BOILED EGGS STUFFED WITH SMOKED SALMON MOUSSE

When hard-cooking eggs, add salt to the water to give it a buoyant, ocean-like quality. The salt makes it easier, afterward, to remove the shell.

Bring water with eggs to a boil, lower heat, and simmer for 12 minutes. Immediately rinse under cold running water; this makes it easier to peel the shell and membrane from the egg.

This appetizer calls for 4 hard-boiled eggs with the yolks removed. We suggest you reserve the yolks and use them to make a sandwich spread for the next day's use. Mash the 4 egg yolks with some chopped onion, parsley, and mayonnaise; season with salt and pepper and spread on dark rye or pumpernickel.

Serves 4.

¾ cup	unsalted butter, softened	175 mL
3 ounces	smoked salmon	100 g
1 tablespoon	lemon juice	15 mL
	Freshly ground white pepper	
¼ cup	heavy (35%) cream	50 mL
1 tablespoon	capers	15 mL
1 tablespoon	chopped fresh chives OR finely sliced scallion (green onion)	15 mL
4	hard-boiled eggs, halved, yolks removed	4
2	slices lemon, rind removed, cut into quarters	2
8	sprigs dill	8

1. In a bowl, beat butter until light.
2. In a food processor fitted with steel blade, or a blender, purée salmon.
3. Combine butter, salmon, lemon juice, and white pepper. Mix gently but thoroughly.
4. In a separate bowl, whip cream. Fold half the whipped cream into salmon mixture. Then fold in remaining whipped cream.
5. Place mixture in pastry bag with large decorator tip.
6. Evenly divide and place capers and chives in hollow of each half egg. Cover with salmon mousse, mounding mixture high and with a spiral (as is done with soft ice cream).

7. Insert ¼ slice lemon into each mousse mound (so it resembles a biscuit stuck into ice cream sundae), and garnish with sprig of dill.

SOFT-BOILED EGG IN ASPIC WITH NOVA SCOTIA SALMON

An easy-to-prepare-ahead dish that is elegant and yet inexpensive because you can stretch 2 ounces (60 g) of smoked salmon to serve 4. Eggs should be cooked until they hold their shape when peeled—but do not hard boil.

This recipe calls for small, individual serving cups or ramekins. Ours measure 2 inches (5 cm) in depth and 3½ inches (9 cm) in diameter.

Yield: 4 hors d'oeuvre.

4	large eggs	4
2 cups	cold water	500 mL
2 tablespoons	salt	30 mL
1¾ cups	chicken stock	425 mL
6	sprigs fresh dill	6
1	envelope unflavoured gelatin dissolved in 2 tablespoons (30 mL) cool chicken stock	1
¼ cup	dry sherry	50 mL
2 ounces	sliced smoked salmon	60 g

1. Place eggs, water, and salt in a small saucepan. Heat to boiling, lower heat and simmer 7 minutes. Remove eggs, run under cold water to stop cooking, and peel while still warm. Chill.
2. To make aspic, bring chicken stock and 2 sprigs of dill to boil in a small pot. Add gelatin dissolved in chicken stock and stir well. Remove from heat, add sherry, and discard dill. Let mixture cool but not set.
3. Into each of 4 serving cups or ramekins, pour 2 tablespoons (30 mL) aspic. Chill in refrigerator for 1 hour Keep remaining aspic warm enough not to set.
4. In each cup, place 1 sprig dill on top of aspic. Cover with thin salmon slice trimmed to fit ramekin. Top salmon with egg. Fill each cup to brim with remaining aspic. Refrigerate until aspic is firm. To serve, dip ramekin into warm water for 5 seconds to unmould. Turn upside down to serve.

ARTICHOKES VINAIGRETTE

Artichokes are known not only for their taste, but for their waste. It always amazes me that there's more artichoke after you've eaten it than before. After you've nibbled off the edible meat, the leaves make a pile far larger than the original artichoke.

Serves 4.

4	medium-sized globe artichokes	4
	Juice of ½ lemon	
½ teaspoon	thyme	2 mL
2 tablespoons	salt	30 mL

VINAIGRETTE:

6 tablespoons	olive oil	90 mL
2 tablespoons	cider vinegar	30 mL
½ teaspoon	salt	2 mL
½ teaspoon	freshly ground pepper	2 mL
1 tablespoon	finely chopped shallots OR onion	15 mL
1 teaspoon	chopped fresh parsley	5 mL
½ teaspoon	dry mustard	2 mL
½ teaspoon	finely chopped fresh tarragon OR 1 teaspoon (5 mL) dried tarragon	2 mL

1. Rinse artichokes well under running water. Cut stem off flush with base, trim discoloured leaves, and cut off top third of each artichoke to remove spiny tips. Rub cut edges with lemon to prevent discolouring. Place artichokes in a large stainless-steel or enameled pot. Add water to cover, lemon juice, thyme, and salt.
2. Bring to boil, cover, and cook for 15 to 30 minutes, or until tender. Remove artichokes and stand on heads to drain. Chill.
3. To make vinaigrette, combine all ingredients in a bowl. Mix well. Refrigerate until serving.
4. To serve, spread leaves of artichoke, pull out or scoop out the thistle, or "choke," and fill hollow with vinaigrette. Or, serve vinaigrette on the side.

CREAM OF SMOKED SALMON
FINGER SANDWICHES

*A fancy appetizer that takes only minutes to prepare, yet will
be the dish that guests talk about for days.*
   Ideal for afternoon teas.
   Yield: 9 narrow finger sandwiches.

3 ounces	smoked salmon	100 g
1 teaspoon	olive oil	5 mL
1 teaspoon	chopped chives OR finely sliced scallion (green onion)	5 mL
1 teaspoon	chopped fresh dill	5 mL
	Coarsely ground pepper	
2 tablespoons	sour cream	30 mL
	Salt	
¼ cup	softened butter, unsalted	50 mL
6	slices whole-wheat OR rye bread	6
	Dill sprigs to garnish	

1. In a food processor fitted with steel blade, purée salmon
   with olive oil. (Olive oil helps heighten the flavour of this
   creamy spread.) Alternatively, mash together salmon and
   oil and pass through fine sieve.
2. Add chives, dill, pepper, and sour cream. Mix thoroughly.
   Salt to taste.
3. Butter 6 slices of bread; spread salmon mixture evenly
   over 3 slices and cover with remaining slices.
4. Cut crusts off all 3 sandwiches. Chill at least 30 minutes
   before serving.
5. Prior to serving, pile three sandwiches on top of one
   another; slice into thirds, producing 9 fingers of equal
   width. Arrange on serving dish and garnish each finger
   sandwich with sprig of dill.

FLIN FLON
WHOLE-WHEAT LADYFINGERS

These are wholesome cookies for parties, Christmas and Easter entertaining.

Yield: 40 to 45 ladyfingers.

LADYFINGERS:

³/₄ cup	unsalted butter	175 mL
¹/₃ cup	brown sugar	75 mL
2 tablespoons	honey	30 mL
¹/₄ cup	sour cream	50 mL
¹/₄ cup	heavy (35%) cream	50 mL
	Pinch of salt	
	Peel of 1 lemon OR orange, grated	
1 teaspoon	vanilla	5 mL
1 teaspoon	baking powder	5 mL
2 ¹/₃ cups	whole-wheat flour	575 mL
1 cup	ground hazelnuts	250 mL
²/₃ cup	pitted dates, chopped very fine	150 mL

GLAZE:

¹/₂ cup	icing sugar	125 mL
1¹/₂ tablespoons	hot orange OR lemon juice	20 mL
¹/₂ teaspoon	melted butter	2 mL

1. Preheat oven to 350°F (180°C).
2. In a bowl, cream together butter and sugar. Add honey, sour cream, and heavy cream. Beat until well mixed and light.
3. Add salt, grated peel, and vanilla. Blend thoroughly.
4. In a separate bowl, mix together baking powder and flour. Gradually add to batter and blend in thoroughly. Fold in hazelnuts and dates.
5. On a well-dusted surface, roll out dough to ¹/₂-inch (1.5-cm) thickness. Dust dough lightly with flour and roll it around rolling pin. Unroll on a well-buttered cookie sheet.
6. Cut rectangular fingers, each 4 × ¹/₂ inch (10 × 1.5 cm), out of dough; remove dough between ladyfingers (they should not be touching) and recombine to form new clump of dough. This can be rolled out again to make more ladyfingers while first batch is in oven.

7. Bake 10 to 15 minutes.
8. To make glaze, combine all ingredients and mix until smooth. Brush ladyfingers with glaze while still warm. Let cool.

SIMPLE PICKLED MUSHROOMS

The flavourful marinade will not only leave guests tickled pink, it'll leave vegetables pickled pink. Especially if you use a good wine vinegar. Don't overcook mushrooms. They should remain firm.
Serves 6 as an appetizer.

1 pound	mushrooms	450 g
½	medium-sized onion, quartered	½
3	cloves garlic, crushed	3
½ teaspoon	black peppercorns	2 mL
1 teaspoon	salt	5 mL
¼ teaspoon	oregano	1 mL
1	bay leaf	1
¼ teaspoon	thyme	1 mL
¼ teaspoon	coriander seeds	1 mL
1	slice lemon	1
1 teaspoon	sugar	5 mL
1 tablespoon	olive oil	15 mL
¼ cup	wine vinegar	50 mL
1½ cups	water	375 mL

1. Remove stems from mushrooms (and save them for a family salad).
2. In a saucepan, combine all ingredients except mushroom caps. Bring to boil. Boil 5 minutes.
3. Add mushrooms. Reduce heat to medium and cook 3 additional minutes. Remove from heat. Chill. (Mushrooms and marinade may be stored in sealed container in refrigerator for up to a week.) Serve slightly chilled or at room temperature.

COLD TERRINE OF SUMMER
VEGETABLES WITH DILL SAUCE

This recipe will dazzle your in-laws, leave your guests gaga, and get you invited to lots of gourmet dinners.

There are a lot of ingredients, yes, but the method is straightforward. The result is an appetizer that not only looks original, but tastes original. Any seasonal vegetables may be used including artichoke bottoms, asparagus, or Swiss chard.

We use a rectangular loaf pan that measures 11 ½ × 4 ½ × 2 ¾ inches (2.2 L). In such a pan, the yield is 24 slices of vegetable terrine.

Serves 12.

TERRINE:

½ pound	carrots, cut lengthwise into thin strips	225 g
1	stalk celery, cut lengthwise into 3 strips	1
½ pound	leeks, white and light green part only, washed well and split in half lengthwise	225 g
½ pound	green beans, ends trimmed	225 g
½	red pepper, cut lengthwise into thin strips	½
4	whole scallions (green onions)	4
1	medium-sized zucchini, cut lengthwise into thin strips	1
½	rutabaga (yellow turnip), peeled, cut into thin strips	½
½ pound	fresh spinach, stalks removed	225 g
4 cups	chicken stock	1 L
	Salt and pepper	
¼ cup	unflavoured gelatin	50 mL
¼ cup	dry Canadian sherry	50 mL
¼ cup	cold water	50 mL
1 teaspoon	coarsely ground pepper	5 mL

DILL SAUCE:

½ cup	sour cream	125 mL
½ cup	mayonnaise	125 mL
1 teaspoon	chopped dill OR chervil	5 mL
1 teaspoon	chopped parsley	5 mL

1 teaspoon	Dijon mustard	5 mL
	Juice of ½ lemon	
1 teaspoon	finely chopped chives OR thinly sliced scallion (green onion)	5 mL
	Salt and freshly ground pepper	

1. To make terrine, wash all vegetables well. Steam or boil each vegetable, *except spinach*, individually in chicken stock, well seasoned with salt and pepper, until tender but still firm.
2. Drain each vegetable and rinse immediately in cold running water to set colour and stop cooking. Drain and chill vegetable. Set aside. Reserve chicken stock and let cool slightly.
3. To prepare spinach, wash well, removing all sand. Do not shake off excess water. Without adding additional water, place in saucepan over low heat; cook, covered, until tender. Remove, squeeze out excess water, and chill.
4. To make aspic, dissolve gelatin in mixture of sherry and cold water. Let stand about 10 minutes. Stir. Add gelatin mixture to warm, but not boiling, chicken stock. Season with salt to taste. Stir well. Strain through cheesecloth and let aspic cool, but not harden.
5. Coat bottom of terrine mould or loaf pan with thin, even layer of aspic. Fully cover with layer of spinach. Evenly spread a few spoonsful of aspic to cover spinach.(This is the start of a multi-layered loaf.) Sprinkle with black pepper.
6. Lay carrots in strips, buttressed end to end, running length of mould. Make as many full rows (lengthwise) as supply permits.
7. Cover with thin film of aspic. Repeat procedure using all vegetables, alternating with layers of aspic. Crown loaf with final layer of aspic.
8. Chill terrine at least 5 hours before serving.
9. To unmould, dip loaf pan in warm water for 5 to 15 seconds. Turn upside down to serve. To cut, use a razor-sharp knife that has been dipped in warm water; cut slices about ½ inch (1.5 cm) thick.
10. To make dill sauce, combine all sauce ingredients and mix well. If sauce is too thick, dilute with 1 or 2 tablespoons (15 or 30 mL) cold water. Season to taste. Serve with slices of chilled terrine.

PERFECT PÂTÉ MAISON

Wherever Tony goes, people ask him for one of his delicious pâté recipes. Over the years, this simple but tasty recipe has evolved.

You may use one, two, or even three rectangular pâté moulds or loaf pans, whatever's large enough to accommodate 3 pounds of liver.

Pâté is best when made well in advance. By letting it sit for a day or two, you allow the spices and wines a chance to work together, creating something that is larger in flavour than the sum of the parts.

Yield: 3 pounds (1.3 kg) pâté.

3 pounds	chicken livers	1.3 kg
2 cups	lard	500 mL
1	clove garlic	1
½ teaspoon	freshly ground white pepper	2 mL
¼ teaspoon	cinnamon	1 mL
¼ teaspoon	ground cloves	1 mL
2 tablespoons	brandy	30 mL
2 tablespoons	Madeira	30 mL
1 teaspoon	powdered chicken stock	5 mL
2	egg yolks	2
	Sufficient bacon to line pâté mould(s), strips laid across width of mould(s), *not* the length	
3	bay leaves	3
	Chopped aspic to garnish	

1. Preheat oven to 400°F (200°C).
2. Pass raw chicken livers and lard together through meat grinder at least 5 times.
3. On last pass, add garlic. Divide liver-fat mixture into small, workable portions; place small batches in blender or food processor fitted with steel blade. Purée mixture until smooth and creamy.
4. In a bowl, combine liver-fat purée with white pepper, cinnamon, cloves, brandy, Madeira, powdered chicken stock, and egg yolks. Mix well with wooden spoon.
5. Place strips of bacon across the bottom and up the sides of each rectangular loaf pan. (Drape strips across width; the bottom and sides should be fully covered and there should be sufficiently long ends left to fold over pâté loaf.)

6. Fill mould(s) about ³/₄ full with pâté mixture. Fold ends of bacon strips across top of loaf. Place a bay leaf on top of each bacon-wrapped loaf for garnish.
7. Set mould(s) in pan containing 1 inch (2.5 cm) water and place in oven. (The water bath ensures an even, moist, slow heat.) Bake 1 hour uncovered; but if bacon colours too quickly, cover with foil and complete cooking.
8. Remove from oven. Set a weighted loaf pan or similar heavy object directly on top of each baked loaf to displace fat. Allow to cool overnight. Refrigerate for later use. Decorate slices with chopped aspic.

EGGS AND
LUNCHEON DISHES

SELKIRK SPINACH QUICHE

Serves 4 to 6.

	Dough for 9-inch (1-L) pie shell (page 207)	
1	10-ounce (285-g) bag spinach	1
1 ½ teaspoons	salt	7 mL
1 tablespoon	unsalted butter	15 mL
3	scallions (green onions), thinly sliced	3
½	clove garlic, finely chopped	½
6	mushrooms, thinly sliced	6
3	large eggs	3
1 cup	heavy (35%) cream	250 mL
⅛ teaspoon	freshly grated nutmeg	0.5 mL
1 teaspoon	powdered chicken stock, diluted in 1 tablespoon (15 mL) water	5 mL
¾ cup	¼-inch (0.75-cm) cubes Canadian Emmenthal cheese	175 mL
	Paprika	

1. Preheat oven to 400°F (200°C).
2. Line a 9-inch (1-L) pie pan with pastry dough.
3. Trim and discard spinach stems. Wash leaves well; do not shake off excess water. Place in saucepan over medium heat. Add 1 teaspoon (5 mL) salt; cover and steam for about 1 minute. Drain and chop coarsely. Set aside.
4. In a sauté pan, melt butter over medium heat. When foam subsides, sauté scallions, garlic, and mushrooms until scallions are soft. Combine with spinach, mix thoroughly, and set aside.
5. In a separate bowl, beat eggs with cream for 1 minute. Add remaining salt, nutmeg, and diluted chicken stock. Mix well.
6. To prepare quiche, spread spinach-mushroom mixture evenly over pie shell. Cover with a layer of diced cheese. Cover with egg-cream mixture. Sprinkle lightly with paprika.
7. Bake 40 minutes, or until custard is firm.

BEST-EVER QUICHE LORRAINE

Everyone's got a version of this custardy pie; but Tony sets his apart from others with a secret touch: a pinch of Ac'cent. He also prefers to substitute ham for bacon—the traditional filling. As well, ours is a time-saver's shortcut quiche: it doesn't require a prebaked pie shell. Tony says this is an unnecessary step if you use our pâte brisée dough (page 207). You may prebake by lining the shell with foil and beans and bake in a 400°F (200°C) oven for 10 minutes if you're from the old school. But it's not necessary.

Serves 4 to 6.

	Dough for 9-inch (1-L) pie shell (page 207)	
2 cups	table (18%) cream	500 mL
4	eggs	4
	Salt and freshly ground pepper	
½ teaspoon	freshly grated nutmeg	2 mL
	Pinch of Ac'cent	
½ cup	finely diced ham	125 mL
1 cup	finely diced Canadian Emmenthal cheese	250 mL
	Paprika	

1. Preheat oven to 450°F (230°C).
2. Line a 9-inch (1-L) pie pan with pastry dough.
3. In a bowl, combine cream, eggs, salt, pepper, nutmeg, and Ac'cent and beat well.
4. Cover bottom of pie shell with ham and diced cheese. Cover with egg-cream mixture. Sprinkle with paprika.
5. Bake about 35 minutes, or until custard is firm.

GREEN PEPPER AND EGG SANDWICH SPREAD

An original, tasty spread for the tired-of-eating-peanut-butter-sandwich crowd and those who brown-bag it to work every day.

Yield: 2 cups (500 mL).

2	green OR red peppers	2
1 tablespoon	olive oil	15 mL
4	hard-boiled eggs	4
1 teaspoon	tarragon vinegar OR 1/8 teaspoon (0.5 mL) tarragon mixed with 1 teaspoon (5 mL) vinegar	5 mL
1 1/2 teaspoons	salt	7 mL
1	medium-sized tomato, peeled, seeded	1
4	anchovy fillets	4
1/4 teaspoon	oregano	1 mL
1/2	small onion	1/2
1/2 teaspoon	dry mustard	2 mL
1/2 teaspoon	soy sauce	2 mL
1/4 teaspoon	freshly ground pepper	1 mL

1. Rub peppers with oil. Place under preheated broiler and grill until skin is dark, crisp, and puffy. Turn often to prevent total burning. Remove from oven.
2. Rub skin off using towel. Cut peppers in half and remove seeds.
3. In a blender or a food processor fitted with steel blade, combine all ingredients including peppers. Purée until smooth. Chill before serving.

POTATO OMELETTE

Serves 4.

3 tablespoons	oil	45 mL
4	medium-sized potatoes, peeled, quartered, thinly sliced	4
1 1/2 teaspoons	salt	7 mL
3 tablespoons	finely chopped onion	45 mL
1	clove garlic, finely chopped	1
2 tablespoons	chopped parsley	30 mL
3	large eggs	3
	Freshly ground pepper	
1/4 cup	grated Canadian Emmenthal cheese	50 mL
1 teaspoon	oil	5 mL

1. In a large sauté pan, heat oil over medium heat. Sauté potatoes with 1 teaspoon (5 mL) salt, about 20 minutes, or until lightly golden. Turn potatoes with spatula to prevent burning.
2. Add onion and sauté 5 additional minutes.
3. Add garlic and parsley and turn with spatula until well combined. Remove from heat.
4. In a separate bowl, beat eggs, 1/2 teaspoon (2 mL) salt, and pepper to taste; add grated cheese and mix well.
5. Transfer potato mixture to a lightly oiled omelette pan over medium-high heat. When hot, add egg mixture. Flatten with spatula. Cook until partially set, about 3 minutes, or until edges are firm.
6. Cover pan with large plate (face down) and flip, transferring omelette to plate. Slide omelette from plate back into pan. Cook 3 additional minutes or until done. Serve hot or cold.

RED EGGS
IN A GOLDEN NEST

An original, easy-to-make dish that is a hit with kids for breakfast, yet stylish enough to impress company.
Serves 2.

4	slices whole-wheat OR white bread	4
2 tablespoons	unsalted butter	30 mL
4	eggs, separated, yolks kept whole and separate from each other	4
¼ cup	grated medium Canadian Cheddar cheese (orange colour)	50 mL
4	slices ham	4
4 teaspoons	ketchup	20 mL
	Salt and freshly ground pepper	
2 teaspoons	unsalted butter	10 mL

1. Preheat oven to 400° F (200°C).
2. Remove crust from bread. Toast and butter slices and set aside.
3. In a bowl, beat egg whites until stiff. Gently fold in grated Cheddar.
4. Place one slice ham on each buttered piece of toast. Cover with a thick layer of egg-cheese mixture. Form a well in centre of mixture using back of a spoon. Into each hollow place 1 teaspoon (5 mL) ketchup.
5. Gently slide 1 whole egg yolk into each hollow. Salt and pepper to taste. Top each yolk with ½ teaspoon (2 mL) butter.
6. Bake 8 minutes, or until egg whites are slightly golden but not dried out. Serve hot.

TOUCHDOWN CHEESE SPREAD

It's Sunday afternoon, your team has just scored a touchdown and you've got enough time to raid the refrigerator. If you've made our mayonnaise-cheese spread in advance, all you've got to do is smear it on some crusty French bread, give it a minute under the broiler, and voilà, you're back at the 50-yard line (no metrics, please!) for the resumption of play.

Yield: 1 cup (250 mL).

½ cup	mayonnaise	125 mL
⅓ cup	grated Canadian Emmenthal cheese	75 mL
2 tablespoons	grated Parmesan cheese	30 mL
1 tablespoon	very finely chopped onion	15 mL
1	clove garlic, very finely chopped	1
	Freshly ground pepper	
⅛ teaspoon	thyme	0.5 mL
8 to 10	slices French bread	8 to 10

1. In a bowl, combine all ingredients except French bread. Mix thoroughly. Refrigerate for later use.
2. Spread bread slices evenly with cheese mixture; place under preheated broiler for 1 minute or until golden in colour. Serve at once. Touchdown!

SOUPS

CREAM OF JERUSALEM ARTICHOKE SOUP

Contrary to its name, the Jerusalem artichoke is neither from Jerusalem nor is it, in any way, related to the common globe artichoke that most of us know. In fact, the Jerusalem artichoke originated in North America! Champlain found Indians growing these tall (6- to 12-foot-high) plants when he reached our shores.

The edible part is the underground tuber, a knobbly thing resembling a potato. It's available in wintery months in ethnic food stores. Buy firm tubers with clean skins, free from mould or blemishes.

Our artichoke tubers were transported to the Old World in the early 1600s. Before they left Canada, they were called poires de terre (earth pears); by the time they reached England they were being called Jerusalem artichokes.

Some suggest this is a corruption, or aural translation, of what Italians called the vegetable: girasole – which sounds something like Jerusalem. It means sunflower – which is what the plant is.

Call it what you like, our creamy soup is dreamy.

Yield: 6 cups (1.5 L).

1 tablespoon	unsalted butter	15 mL
1	large onion, finely chopped	1
3	medium-sized potatoes, peeled, sliced	3
1½ teaspoons	finely chopped parsley	7 mL
1 teaspoon	thyme	5 mL
4	large Jerusalem artichokes (about 1 pound), peeled, sliced	4
5 cups	chicken stock	1.2 L
½ cup	heavy (35%) cream	125 mL
	Salt	

1. Melt butter in a saucepan over medium heat. When foam subsides, sauté onion until transparent.
2. Add potatoes, parsley, thyme, artichokes, and chicken stock. Bring to boil. Reduce heat and simmer, covered, about 30 minutes or until potatoes are tender.

3. Transfer mixture to blender or food processor fitted with steel blade and purée until smooth or strain through fine sieve.
4. Return soup to saucepan. Add cream and salt. Bring to boil. Serve at once, or refrigerate and serve later, chilled.

TRANS-CANADA APPLE-ONION BISQUE

The apples come from the Okanagan Valley in British Columbia. The onions come from Bradford, Ontario. And together they meet in this delicious soup.

Yield: 4 cups (1 L).

2 tablespoons	unsalted butter	30 mL
2 cups	chopped onion	500 mL
2 cups	peeled, cored, chopped Golden Delicious apples	500 mL
1	clove garlic, crushed	1
½ teaspoon	chopped fresh OR dried thyme	2 mL
1	bay leaf	1
½ teaspoon	freshly ground pepper	2 mL
1 teaspoon	coriander seeds, crushed OR ground	5 mL
4 cups	chicken stock	1 L
¼ cup	heavy (35%) cream	50 mL
	Salt	
1 tablespoon	chopped fresh mint	15 mL

1. Melt butter in a saucepan over medium heat. When foam subsides, sauté onion, apple, garlic, thyme, bay leaf, pepper, and coriander 10 minutes, or until onion is lightly browned.
2. Add chicken stock. Bring to boil, reduce heat and simmer, covered, 15 minutes.
3. Add cream and simmer 1 additional minute. Add salt. Purée in blender or food processor, or strain through fine sieve. Serve hot or cold.
4. Sprinkle with chopped mint before serving.

BUDGET BEAN AND TURNIP SOUP

A hearty soup for a cold winter's day. This one's got all the seasonings that set Tony's Spanish taste buds tingling.
Yield: 8 cups (2 L).

1 pound	lima beans	450 g
12 cups	cold water	3 L
2 tablespoons	unsalted butter	30 mL
1	onion, chopped	1
2	tomatoes, peeled, seeded, diced	2
1	¹/₂-pound (225-g) piece salted pork belly	1
¹/₂ teaspoon	thyme	2 mL
¹/₂	head (bulb) of garlic	¹/₂
1	turnip, peeled, quartered	1
2 teaspoons	powdered chicken stock	10 mL
¹/₄ teaspoon	freshly ground pepper	1 mL
¹/₂ teaspoon	salt	2 mL

1. Rinse beans and drain. Place 6 cups (1.5 L) cold water in a large pot; add beans. Bring to boil. Reduce heat and simmer 2 minutes. Remove from heat and let stand 1 hour. Drain beans and set aside.
2. Melt butter in a large saucepan over medium heat. When foam subsides, sauté onion until soft. Add tomatoes and cook 1 additional minute.
3. Add all other ingredients, including drained beans and remaining 6 cups (1.5 L) cold water. Bring to boil. Reduce heat and simmer, covered, about 1¹/₄ hours. Slice pork into pieces and divide among bowls; pour soup and serve hot.

CHILLED GREEN BEAN SOUP

This recipe has been in my family for longer than anyone can remember. I got it from my grandmother, Myra, but where she got it is anyone's guess.

To make it fancier, cut the green beans Chinese style – on the diagonal.

It can be served hot, but I prefer mine well chilled.

Serves 4.

½ teaspoon	salt	2 mL
1½ cups	water	375 mL
1 pound	green beans, ends trimmed, cut into 1-inch (2.5-cm) pieces	450 g
1	egg, beaten with 2 tablespoons (30 mL) water	1
	Juice of ½ lemon	
1 cup	sour cream	250 mL
	Salt and freshly ground pepper	

1. Bring salted water to a boil. Cook green beans about 5 minutes or until just tender. *Beans must stay crunchy.* Drain, reserving cooking water.
2. Place beaten egg in a bowl. Add warm water from cooked beans, beating constantly to prevent egg from curdling.
3. Add lemon juice and sour cream. Mix well. Salt and pepper to taste. Add cooked beans. Cover and refrigerate. Serve chilled.

CHILLED CUCUMBER AND TOMATO SOUP

Yield: 4 cups (1 L).

2	medium-sized cucumbers	2
2	medium-sized tomatoes, peeled, seeded	2
½ teaspoon	Worcestershire sauce	2 mL
2 tablespoons	chopped fresh mint	30 mL
1	clove garlic	1
1 cup	chicken stock	250 mL
1 tablespoon	oil	15 mL
1 cup	sour cream	250 mL
2 tablespoons	finely chopped onion	30 mL

1. Peel cucumbers, cut in half lengthwise, and scoop out seeds with a teaspoon. Dice one quarter of 1 cucumber for garnish and reserve. Chop remaining cucumber into pieces and place in blender or food processor fitted with steel blade; add tomatoes, Worcestershire sauce, 1 tablespoon (15 mL) mint, and garlic. Purée until smooth.
2. Add chicken stock, oil, and sour cream. Mix well.
3. Transfer soup to serving bowl. Add reserved diced cucumber and onion. Chill well.
4. To serve, garnish with remaining mint, finely chopped.

LEMON AND EGG SOUP

A slurping cousin to Greece's avgolemono, this soup can be served hot or chilled.

Yield: 4 cups (1 L).

2	eggs	2
	Juice of 1 lemon	
4 cups	boiling, well-seasoned chicken stock	1 L
	Salt and freshly ground white pepper	
2 teaspoons	chopped fresh mint OR coriander	10 mL

1. In a large bowl, beat eggs with wire whisk until light and frothy. Slowly add lemon juice, beating constantly.
2. In a slow, steady trickle, add half the boiling chicken stock, beating constantly with whisk until ingredients are well blended.
3. Slowly add remaining chicken stock, beating until fully blended. Season to taste with salt and white pepper.
4. Serve hot or chilled. Garnish with mint or coriander.

CHILLED CARROT AND YOGURT SOUP WITH MINT

A simple, refreshing summer soup created especially for The Best of Canada.
Yield: 5 cups (1.2 L).

2 tablespoons	unsalted butter	30 mL
½ cup	chopped onion	125 mL
1⅔ cups	sliced carrots	400 mL
1	bay leaf	1
½ teaspoon	thyme	2 mL
	Freshly ground pepper	
1⅔ cups	thinly sliced, peeled potatoes	400 mL
4 cups	chicken stock	1 L
¾ cup	yogurt (*not* skim-milk variety)	175 mL
	Salt	
5 teaspoons	finely chopped fresh mint	25 mL

1. Melt butter in a saucepan or casserole, over medium heat. When foam subsides, add onion, carrots, bay leaf, thyme, and pepper to taste. Cook, covered, 4 minutes.
2. Add potatoes and chicken stock. Cook, covered, 30 minutes.
3. Transfer mixture to food processor fitted with steel blade. Purée until smooth. Strain through fine sieve.
4. Add yogurt and salt. Mix well. Refrigerate.
5. Garnish each serving with 1 teaspoon (5 mL) finely chopped mint.

P.E.I. MUSSEL SOUP

Serves 4.

2 tablespoons	olive oil	30 mL
¾ cup	finely chopped onion	175 mL
½ teaspoon	thyme	2 mL
1	clove garlic, crushed	1
1	bay leaf	1
½ teaspoon	freshly ground pepper	2 mL
1	small tomato, chopped	1
48	mussels, scrubbed, debearded (page 64)	48
1 cup	dry white wine	250 mL
1 tablespoon	unsalted butter	15 mL
¼ cup	thinly sliced leek (white and light green portion only)	50 mL
1 tablespoon	finely diced, peeled turnip	15 mL
2 tablespoons	small carrot sticks	30 mL
2 tablespoons	finely diced celery	30 mL
1 tablespoon	finely chopped parsley	15 mL
¼ teaspoon	sage	1 mL
3 cups	cold water	750 mL
1 teaspoon	Pernod	5 mL
¼ cup	heavy (35%) cream	50 mL

1. In a large saucepan, heat oil over medium heat. Sauté onion until soft. Add thyme, garlic, bay leaf, pepper, and tomato and cook 3 to 4 additional minutes.
2. Add mussels and white wine. Cover and increase heat to high. Cook 9 to 10 minutes, or until mussels open. Remove from heat.
3. Remove mussels and cut meat from shells. Discard shells. Set meat aside. Strain stock and reserve.
4. In a saucepan over medium heat, melt butter. When foam subsides, sauté leek, turnip, carrot, and celery, about 7 minutes or until vegetables are soft.
5. Add parsley, sage, strained mussel stock, and cold water. Bring to boil.
6. Add Pernod, reduce heat and simmer, uncovered, 20 minutes.
7. Add cooked mussels and cream. Simmer, covered, 3 additional minutes. (Don't cook longer or mussels will get tough and stringy. No salt is required as mussels are themselves salty.) Serve at once.

TOMATO AND TARRAGON SOUP

Yield: 4 cups (1 L).

½ cup	unsalted butter	125 mL
1⅓ cups	chopped onion	325 mL
1	28-ounce (800-mL) can tomatoes	1
½ cup	dry white wine	125 mL
1 tablespoon	sugar	15 mL
1 teaspoon	dried tarragon	5 mL
	Salt and freshly ground pepper	
¼ cup	heavy (35%) cream	50 mL
	Sour cream	

1. In a sauté pan over medium heat, melt butter. Sauté onion until golden. Chop tomatoes coarsely and add with can liquid to onions. Heat thoroughly. Add white wine, sugar, and tarragon. Stir well. Reduce heat and simmer, covered, 30 minutes.
2. Transfer mixture to blender or food processor fitted with steel blade and purée until smooth. Strain through fine sieve and transfer to saucepan. Season to taste with salt and pepper. Bring to a boil, add cream, and stir through. Serve hot. Garnish each serving with dollop of sour cream.

ONION SOUP WITH SAGE
AU GRATIN

Yield: 4 cups (1 L).

2 tablespoons	unsalted butter	30 mL
3 cups	sliced onions	750 mL
1	bay leaf	1
½ teaspoon	thyme	2 mL
1 teaspoon	chopped fresh sage OR ¼ teaspoon (1 mL) dried	5 mL
½ teaspoon	freshly ground pepper	2 mL
¼ cup	dry white wine	50 mL
2 tablespoons	dry sherry	30 mL
2 cups	canned beef consommé	500 mL
2 cups	cold water	500 mL
1 tablespoon	cornstarch mixed with 3 tablespoons (45 mL) water	15 mL
1 teaspoon	salt	5 mL
	Freshly ground pepper	
4	slices French bread, cut ¼ inch (1 cm) thick	4
¼ cup	grated Gruyère cheese	50 mL
¼ cup	grated Parmesan cheese	50 mL

1. In a saucepan over medium heat, melt butter. When foam subsides, sauté onions with bay leaf, thyme, sage, and pepper about 8 minutes, or until onion is dark brown but not burned.
2. Add wine and sherry; increase heat to high. Deglaze pan and reduce liquid to half.
3. Add consommé and water. Bring to boil. Reduce heat and simmer, uncovered, 20 minutes.
4. Add cornstarch diluted in water and simmer 2 additional minutes. Add salt. Pepper to taste. Keep hot.
5. Place French bread slices under preheated broiler and grill until brown. Flip and brown other side.
6. In a separate bowl, mix Gruyère and Parmesan cheeses.
7. Fill 4 individual-sized earthenware crocks about ¾ full with soup; cover each with a slice of grilled bread and top with 2 tablespoons (25 mL) mixed cheese. Place under broiler until cheese is golden brown. Serve at once.

SORREL SOUP

Sorrel is a romaine-looking plant that packs a taste-wallop larger than anything Popeye ever got from a can of his greens. Sorrel is actually a perennial herb related to the buckwheat family. It has grown in popularity across Canada and is now available in most markets. If you can't find any sorrel, this soup may be made with spinach. The colour will be the same but the taste will be worlds apart.

Yield: 3 cups (750 mL).

1 tablespoon	unsalted butter	15 mL
1	medium-sized onion, chopped	1
½ cup	firmly packed sorrel leaves OR spinach	125 mL
2	medium-sized potatoes, peeled, cut into pieces	2
3 cups	chicken stock	750 mL
	Salt and freshly ground pepper	
2 tablespoons	heavy (35%) cream	30 mL
1 tablespoon	finely chopped sorrel for garnish	15 mL

1. In a saucepan over medium heat, melt butter. When foam subsides, sauté onion until transparent.
2. Add sorrel and sauté 15 additional seconds. Add potatoes and chicken stock. Bring to boil. Reduce heat and simmer, covered, 30 minutes.
3. Transfer mixture to blender or food processor fitted with steel blade. Purée until smooth. Season to taste with salt and pepper.
4. Return soup to saucepan. Bring to boil. Add cream and simmer 1 minute. Garnish with sorrel. Serve hot.

SETTLERS' SOUP

An original creation for The Best of Canada.
Yield: 10 cups (2.5 L).

2 tablespoons	unsalted butter	30 mL
¾ cup	finely chopped onion	175 mL
2	slices bacon, cut into small pieces	2
1½ cups	diced, peeled squash (preferably Hubbard)	375 mL
1 cup	diced, peeled turnip	250 mL
½ teaspoon	thyme	2 mL
	Freshly ground pepper	
1 cup	diced, peeled tomato	250 mL
2 cups	fresh OR canned corn kernels	500 mL
2 tablespoons	chopped parsley	30 mL
8 cups	cold water	2 L
½	3-pound (1.3-kg) chicken, cut lengthwise	½
¼ cup	heavy (35%) cream	50 mL
1 teaspoon	salt	5 mL

1. In a large saucepan over medium heat, melt butter. Sauté onions, bacon, squash, turnip with thyme and pepper, stirring, about 5 minutes.
2. Add tomato and cook 4 additional minutes.
3. Add corn, parsley, water, and chicken. Bring to boil. Reduce heat and simmer, covered, 1 hour. Skim fat off top periodically.
4. Remove chicken. Pick meat from bones; shred meat and return to pot.
5. Add cream and salt. Bring to boil, and boil for 1 minute. Stir. Serve hot.

HUBBARD SQUASH BISQUE

Here's a creamy winter soup made with a dreamy winter squash. An original creation for The Best of Canada.
Yield: 12 cups (3 L).

2 tablespoons	unsalted butter	30 mL
2 cups	chopped onion	500 mL
1	clove garlic, finely chopped	1
1	bay leaf	1
½ teaspoon	thyme	2 mL
½ teaspoon	freshly ground pepper	2 mL
1	tomato, cut into pieces	1
3 pounds	Hubbard squash, peeled, cored, cut into 2-inch (5-cm) cubes	1.3 kg
1	pear, peeled, diced	1
½ teaspoon	tarragon	2 mL
½ teaspoon	mild curry powder	2 mL
8 cups	chicken stock	2 L
¼ cup	heavy (35%) cream	50 mL

1. In a soup pot over medium heat, melt butter. When foam subsides, sauté onion until soft.
2. Add garlic, bay leaf, thyme, and pepper, and sauté for an additional 30 seconds.
3. Add tomato and cook, stirring, 1 additional minute.
4. Add squash, pear, tarragon, and curry powder, cooking 1 additional minute.
5. Add chicken stock. Bring to boil, reduce heat and simmer, covered, 1 hour.
6. Remove bay leaf. Transfer soup to food processor fitted with steel blade or blender; add cream. Blend thoroughly, or strain through fine sieve. Serve at once. (If serving cold, withhold the cream; blend and refrigerate soup. Add cream just before serving, and blend thoroughly. Optionally, for a more diet-conscious potage, eliminate the cream altogether; the bisque is beautiful by itself.)

FISH AND SHELLFISH

NEWFOUNDLAND COD PIE

An original dish with an original flavour. You might never think of serving cod fillets to dinner guests, but this dish is elegant enough to do so. It's also easy enough to prepare for family meals.
Serves 4.

¼ cup	unsalted butter	50 mL
½ cup	finely chopped onion	125 mL
1	clove garlic, finely chopped	1
1 tablespoon	finely chopped parsley	15 mL
1 teaspoon	paprika	5 mL
½ teaspoon	thyme	2 mL
½ teaspoon	salt	2 mL
	Freshly ground pepper	
2 tablespoons	tomato paste	30 mL
½ cup	dry white wine	125 mL
10 ounces	fresh OR frozen cod fillets, cut into a total of 3 or 4 pieces	300 g
2 tablespoons	flour, sifted	30 mL
3 cups	mashed potatoes (page 151)	750 mL
3 tablespoons	grated medium-aged Canadian Cheddar cheese	45 mL

1. In a frying pan over medium heat, melt half the butter. When foam subsides, sauté onion until soft and lightly browned. Add garlic, parsley, paprika, thyme, salt, pepper, and tomato paste. Heat through, stirring.
2. Add white wine. Bring to boil and reduce liquid to half. Remove sauce from heat and set aside.
3. Dredge fillets with flour, coating both sides of each piece. In a separate frying pan over medium heat, melt remaining butter. When foam subsides, sauté fillets until lightly browned. Set aside.
4. In a bowl, thoroughly mix mashed potatoes with grated Cheddar, and transfer mixture to a pastry bag fitted with a decorating tip.
5. Preheat oven to 375°F (190°C).
6. Transfer fillets to a 9-inch (1-L) ovenproof pie plate. Cover with sauce. Cover with mashed potato mixture, generously squeezing mixture out of pastry bag until dish is mounded and fish is fully covered.
7. Bake on middle rack of oven 25 minutes or until potatoes are lightly browned. Serve hot.

COLOURFUL COD CASSEROLE

Serves 4.

¹/₂	red pepper	¹/₂
2	medium-sized potatoes	2
1 tablespoon	oil	15 mL
3	large onions, thinly sliced	3
1	bay leaf	1
1 teaspoon	coarsely crushed pepper	5 mL
1 teaspoon	salt	5 mL
1	clove garlic, finely chopped	1
2¹/₂ cups	canned tomatoes, chopped OR 2 cups (500 mL) fresh tomatoes, peeled, seeded, chopped	625 mL
1¹/₂ teaspoons	powdered chicken stock	7 mL
1 pound	fresh OR frozen cod fillets, thawed	450 g
1 tablespoon	chopped parsley	15 mL
1 cup	frozen OR canned peas	250 mL

1. Cut red pepper lengthwise into very thin strips. Peel potatoes, cut in half and slice thin.
2. In a sauté pan, heat oil over medium heat. Sauté onion until transparent. Add red pepper strips, bay leaf, pepper, and salt. Sauté for an additional 30 seconds.
3. Add garlic, tomatoes, potatoes, and powdered chicken stock. Reduce heat and simmer, uncovered, 20 minutes.
4. Add cod, parsley, and peas. Simmer, covered, an additional 15 minutes. Serve at once.

MAGNIFICENT MUSSELS
WITH SORREL

Rather than the scrawny, wild mussels that most fishmongers sell, we prefer the new, cultivated mussels that are being harvested in P.E.I. These cost about twice the price of old-fashioned, wild mussels, but they're three times as fleshy, and the rate of rejection, once you get them home, is nearly nil.

To prepare mussels, scrub them well and cut off or pull out their beards (those hairy-looking strands that come out of the shell). Some purists like to give their mussels a bath from the inside out—which means putting them in a bucket of cold water with a handful of cornmeal. Let them feed on the cornmeal for about an hour and they'll clean out their innards in the process.

If sorrel, a soury plant with romaine-looking leaves that is gaining popularity across Canada, is not available in your markets, substitute spinach here.

This dish may be served as an appetizer or entrée.
Serves 4 to 8.

3 tablespoons	unsalted butter	45 mL
2 tablespoons	finely chopped onion	30 mL
¼ cup	finely chopped sorrel OR spinach	50 mL
1	bay leaf	1
¼ teaspoon	thyme	1 mL
½ cup	dry white wine	125 mL
¼ teaspoon	freshly ground pepper	1 mL
48	mussels, preferably cultivated variety, scrubbed and debearded	48
1 tablespoon	lemon juice	15 mL
¼ cup	heavy (35%) cream	50 mL
	Salt to taste	

1. In a heavy saucepan over medium heat, melt 1 tablespoon (15 mL) of the butter. When foam subsides, add onion, sorrel, bay leaf, and thyme, cooking slowly until onion is soft and transparent.
2. Add white wine, pepper, and mussels. Cover and steam until all mussels open, about 6 to 8 minutes.
3. Transfer mussels to heated serving platter and discard top shell of each. Reserve pan liquid.
4. Let liquid settle in saucepan for a few minutes; pour slowly into another saucepan. (This will help remove any sand or sediment that mussels may have contained, although this is minimal if they're cultivated.)
5. Add lemon juice and bring sauce to boil. Add cream and reduce liquid to half. Season to taste.
6. Finish sauce by adding 2 tablespoons (30 mL) butter; shake pan back and forth to work butter into heated sauce. Do not boil or butter will separate out and rise to top.
7. Pour sauce over mussels and serve while hot.

GRAND BANKS LOBSTER CRÊPES

Appropriately named, for these crêpes and your neighbour-hood bank have one thing in common: they're both rich.
Yield: 10 crêpes.

2 tablespoons	unsalted butter	30 mL
2 tablespoons	finely chopped onion	30 mL
½ cup	diced mushrooms	125 mL
1	bay leaf	1
	Freshly ground pepper	
10 ounces	freshly boiled (OR canned) lobster meat, cut into ½-inch (1-cm) pieces	300 g
1	clove garlic, finely chopped	1
½ teaspoon	finely chopped tarragon	2 mL
1 teaspoon	paprika	5 mL
¾ cup	dry white wine	175 mL
2 tablespoons	Canadian brandy	30 mL
1 cup	heavy (35%) cream	250 mL
½ teaspoon	salt	2 mL
10	crêpes (page 182)	10
1½ cups	Hollandaise sauce (page 218)	375 mL

1. Melt butter in a sauté pan over medium heat. When foam subsides, sauté onion, mushroom, bay leaf, and pepper until onion is transparent.
2. Add lobster meat, garlic, tarragon, and paprika. Stir and cook 2 additional minutes.
3. Add white wine and brandy. Simmer over low heat and reduce liquid to half.
4. Add cream and salt. Reduce liquid to about ¾ volume, or until sauce coats a wooden spoon.
5. Spoon mixture equally onto 10 prepared crêpes, folding and tucking in ends. Arrange on a serving dish and cover with Hollandaise sauce. If desired, the crêpes may be made in advance and refrigerated. To serve: reheat 20 minutes in a 350°F (180°C) oven and cover with Hollandaise.

NEW BRUNSWICK LOBSTER
AU PERNOD

This dish won Canada's national team a gold medal in the 1972 World Culinary Olympics in Frankfurt, West Germany. Tony was one of our team captains.

Serve the remarkably subtle, sweet meat of lobster over rice pilaf (page 188) or with fluffy white rice.

Serves 4.

¼ cup	unsalted butter	50 mL
14 ounces	uncooked lobster meat, weighed out of shell	400 g
1 teaspoon	finely chopped shallots	5 mL
1 teaspoon	paprika	5 mL
1 teaspoon	finely chopped fresh parsley	5 mL
¼ cup	Pernod	50 mL
1 tablespoon	Canadian brandy	15 mL
1¼ cups	heavy (35%) cream	300 mL
2	egg yolks	2
2 tablespoons	heavy (35%) cream	30 mL
	Salt	
	Cayenne pepper	

1. Melt butter in a sauté pan over medium heat. When foam subsides, sauté lobster until heated through. Remove and set aside.
2. Sauté shallots in same pan until golden brown. Add paprika and return lobster to pan. Add parsley and cook for 1 minute.
3. Add Pernod and brandy, stir, and reduce liquid to half.
4. Add 1¼ cups (300 mL) cream and reduce until sauce evenly coats a spoon.
5. In a separate bowl, mix egg yolks with 2 tablespoons (30 mL) cream and add to pan (this will thicken sauce). Add salt and cayenne pepper to taste. Keep on very low heat until serving. Do not boil, or eggs will be scrambled.

FISHERMAN'S FEAST:
CLAMS IN CREAM SAUCE

You'd almost think hard-shell clams were the product of department-store merchandising: they come in small, medium, and large size. The smallest hard-shell clam is the littleneck. Bigger yet is the cherrystone, and the biggest fellow is the quahog. For this recipe we prefer littlenecks; they tend to be more flavourful.

Clams should be scrubbed well before using. Purists like to clean them inside, too, although it isn't essential. By placing clams in a brine (1/3 cup [75 mL] salt to 16 cups [4 L] of water), and tossing in a little cornmeal (1/4 cup [50 mL] to each 4 cups [1 L] of clams), you'll get the little guys to clean out their insides. They feed on the cornmeal and empty their tummies of all kinds of ocean-floor food.

Serves 2.

1 tablespoon	olive oil	15 mL
2 tablespoons	finely chopped onion OR shallots	30 mL
1/2	tomato, peeled, seeded, diced	1/2
1/2	clove garlic, finely chopped	1/2
1/4 teaspoon	coarsely ground pepper	1 mL
1/4 teaspoon	thyme	1 mL
1	bay leaf	1
24	hard-shell clams, well scrubbed	24
1 teaspoon	finely chopped fresh parsley	5 mL
1/4 cup	dry white wine	50 mL
5 tablespoons	heavy (35%) cream	75 mL
1 teaspoon	lemon juice	5 mL
1	egg yolk	1

1. In a stainless-steel or heavy enameled saucepan, heat oil over medium heat. Sauté onion for 30 seconds.
2. Add tomato and cook for additional 1 minute. Add garlic, pepper, thyme, and bay leaf, and cook for additional 30 seconds.
3. Add clams, parsley, and white wine. Reduce heat and simmer, covered, about 8 minutes or until clams open.
4. Remove clams from liquid, set aside and keep warm. Reduce liquid to half over medium heat. Remove bay leaf. Add 4 tablespoons (60 mL) cream and lemon juice, and reduce again to half.

5. In a small bowl, mix together egg yolk and 1 tablespoon (15 mL) cream. Add clam liquid, stirring constantly. Do not reheat.
6. Place clams on serving platter or individual plates, cover with sauce and serve at once. The dish does not need additional salt; the clams contain enough natural sodium.

SCALLOPS À LA NOUVELLE CUISINE

Serves 2.

8 ounces	scallops	225 g
1 teaspoon	unsalted butter	5 mL
1 tablespoon	finely chopped onion	15 mL
$^1\!/_2$	bay leaf	$^1\!/_2$
12	whole black peppercorns	12
2	tomatoes, chopped	2
$^1\!/_2$ teaspoon	tarragon	2 mL
1	sprig parsley	1
	Pinch of thyme	
1	clove garlic, crushed	1
6 tablespoons	dry white wine	90 mL
$^1\!/_2$ cup	chicken stock	125 mL
$^1\!/_2$ teaspoon	salt	2 mL
	Freshly ground pepper	

1. Rinse scallops and pat dry with paper towels.
2. In a saucepan over medium heat, melt butter. Sauté onion with bay leaf and peppercorns about 30 seconds, or until onion is lightly browned.
3. Add tomatoes, tarragon, parsley, thyme, and garlic. Cook for about 3 minutes.
4. Add wine, increase heat to high, and boil about 2 minutes.
5. Add chicken stock, scallops, and salt. Return to boil, reduce heat, and simmer, covered, about 1 minute. Do not cook scallops longer or they will get tough.
6. Transfer scallops to serving dish. Season sauce with pepper to taste and strain through fine sieve. Mash pulp of tomatoes using wooden spoon and press through sieve. Cover scallops with sauce and serve at once.

PRINCE RUPERT POACHED SALMON

Serves 4.

5 tablespoons	unsalted butter	75 mL
1 tablespoon	finely diced shallots OR onions	15 mL
1 tablespoon	finely diced leeks	15 mL
1 tablespoon	finely diced carrots	15 mL
1 tablespoon	finely diced celery	15 mL
4	6-ounce (180-g) fillets of B.C. salmon, preferably fresh	4
	Salt and freshly ground pepper	
½ cup	dry white wine	125 mL
1¼ cups	heavy (35%) cream OR crème fraîche (page 216)	300 mL
2 teaspoons	chopped fresh parsley	10 mL
	Softened butter	
2	egg yolks	2
¼ cup	queen or king crab meat, shredded	50 mL

1. In a large, flame-proof baking dish, melt 4 tablespoons (60 mL) butter over medium heat. Add shallots, leeks, carrots, and celery; cook, stirring, for 2 minutes.
2. Place salmon fillets over this *mirepoix au maigre*, season with salt and pepper, and pour wine over fish.
3. Pour 1 cup (250 mL) cream over fillets and sprinkle with parsley.
4. Preheat oven to 400°F (200°C).
5. Cut a piece of waxed or parchment paper to fit baking dish. Rub one side with softened butter and place directly on top of fish, buttered side down. Bake for 10 minutes.
6. Remove fish to a serving platter, cover with same waxed paper and keep warm. Transfer liquid and *mirepoix* to a saucepan.
7. Bring liquid to boil over medium heat, and reduce liquid to half or until sauce will coat a wooden spoon. Set aside.
8. In a separate bowl, mix together remaining ¼ cup (50 mL) cream with egg yolks. Add to sauce and stir well, but do not reheat, or eggs may scramble. Salt and pepper to taste.

9. In a small saucepan over medium heat, melt 1 tablespoon (15 mL) butter. Lightly sauté crab meat until heated through.
10. To serve fashionably, coat each dinner plate with sauce. Place salmon fillet on top and garnish each fillet with crab meat.
11. Serve with Pan-Fried Cucumber with Dill (page 147).

ATLANTIC SEAFOOD TRAWLER: SAFFRON SCALLOPS AND SHRIMP

Here is a seductive yet simple seafood dinner for two.
Serves 2.

8	whole scallops	8
2 tablespoons	olive oil	30 mL
8	large shrimp in shells	8
½	onion, finely chopped	½
1	red pepper, diced	1
1	bay leaf	1
	Freshly ground pepper	
1	clove garlic, chopped	1
1	tomato, peeled, seeded, diced	1
½ cup	dry white wine	125 mL
	Pinch of saffron	
	Salt	
1	hard-boiled egg, chopped	1
1 tablespoon	chopped parsley	15 mL

1. Rinse scallops and pat dry with paper towels.
2. In a sauté pan, heat oil over medium heat. Sauté shrimp and scallops lightly, about 1 minute. Remove and set aside.
3. Drain excess oil; add onion, red pepper, bay leaf, and pepper, and sauté about 4 additional minutes.
4. Add garlic and tomato, and cook 2 additional minutes.
5. Return seafood to pan. Add wine and saffron and reduce liquid to half. Salt to taste. Discard bay leaf.
6. Arrange seafood on a serving platter. Sprinkle with chopped egg and parsley. Serve with Lemon and Parsley Rice (page 185).

SCAMPI IN LOVE

Scampi is Italian for a shellfish that is much closer to being a Norwegian lobster than it is to being a prawn or shrimp. They've been served at the Westbury Hotel in Toronto for 20 years and, in many ways, they've put the hotel's dining room on the gourmet circuit.

Many restaurants imitate this famous dish, but none has been able to match Tony's special recipe.

While you'll find uncooked, frozen scampi tails at some fishmongers, we've simplified the recipe by substituting jumbo shrimp, which can be found everywhere.

Serves 2. In love or not.

2 tablespoons	olive oil	30 mL
12	jumbo shrimp, shelled and deveined	12
2	shallots, finely chopped	2
4	mushrooms, thinly sliced	4
2 teaspoons	chopped fresh parsley	10 mL
2 ounces	baby shrimp	60 g
2	cloves garlic, finely chopped	2
	Freshly ground pepper	
2 tablespoons	Courvoisier	30 mL
2 teaspoons	Pernod	10 mL
¾ cup	heavy (35%) cream	175 mL
2 tablespoons	Hollandaise sauce (page 218)	30 mL
	Salt	
2 tablespoons	unsalted butter	30 mL

1. In a sauté pan, heat oil over high heat. Sauté jumbo shrimp very quickly – 1 minute at the most. Remove and set aside.
2. Reduce heat to medium. Add shallots and cook until transparent. Add mushrooms, half the parsley, and cook, stirring, for 30 seconds.
3. Return jumbo shrimp to pan and reserve any juices that may have accumulated while set aside. Add baby shrimp, garlic, and pepper, and cook an additional 30 seconds.
4. Add Courvoisier. In a restaurant, the dish would now be flambéed; however, as this is a potentially hazardous step, we suggest eliminating it unless you are an accomplished flambéer. Add Pernod, cream, and accumulated shrimp juices. Reduce liquid to half over high heat. Sauce should have a velvety consistency. Remove from heat at once.

5. Add Hollandaise sauce and mix well. Season to taste. Incorporate butter in small pieces, juggling pan back and forth, adding a gloss to sauce.
6. Garnish with remaining parsley. At no point return pan to heated burner or Hollandaise will curdle.

SCAMPI IN
TARRAGON CREAM SAUCE

Tony created this dish as corporate chef of the Sutton Place Hotel, Toronto, for TV personality Al Waxman. It has since become a hotel classic.
Serves 2.

2	English cucumbers, peeled	2
2 tablespoons	olive oil	30 mL
10	scampi tails OR jumbo shrimp, shelled and deveined	10
2 teaspoons	finely chopped shallots	10 mL
2	small tomatoes, peeled, cored, diced	2
2	cloves garlic, crushed	2
2 teaspoons	chopped tarragon	10 mL
	Freshly ground pepper	
2 tablespoons	Canadian brandy	30 mL
½ cup	heavy (35%) cream	125 mL
	Salt and pepper	

1. In a large pot of boiling, salted water, blanch peeled cucumbers for 1 minute. Drain and rinse under cold running water to set colour. Drain. Quarter each cucumber lengthwise, and cut quarters into ½-inch (1.5-cm) slices.
2. In a sauté pan, heat oil over medium heat. Sauté scampi lightly, about 1 minute.
3. Add shallots and cucumber, stirring mixture thoroughly. Sauté less than 1 minute.
4. Add tomato, garlic, tarragon, and lots of freshly ground pepper. Cook 1 additional minute.
5. Add brandy and cream and reduce liquid until thick enough to coat a wooden spoon. Salt and pepper to taste.
6. Serve with Spinach and Pear Purée (page 153).

PAUPIETTES QUÉBÉCOISES: FILLETS OF SOLE STUFFED WITH SORREL

Paupiette is a French culinary term that refers to rolling up, in pancake fashion, thin slices of fish or meat that have been lined, or filled, with forcemeat.

For The Best of Canada, Tony has created Paupiettes québécoises – thin fillets of sole lined with sorrel (or with spinach) that are rolled up and secured with toothpicks. The rolled-up fillets, with their spiral of green sorrel showing at the ends, look more like bedrolls than dinner for two. But they're delicious.

Our recipe calls for sole, a member of the flounder family. Fresh fish is preferable, but frozen will do. Baby halibut and turbot – also members of the flounder family – make excellent fillets for this dish, too.

Sorrel is a romaine-looking plant that is slightly sour to the taste. Growing in popularity in Canada, it is available in most markets. If you have difficulty obtaining sorrel for this recipe, spinach may be substituted. The end product looks identical, but sorrel's special flavour will be lacking.

Serves 2.

14	sorrel leaves OR 24 spinach leaves	14
6 cups	water	1.5 L
	Salt	
6	small fillets of sole	6
½ teaspoon	salt	2 mL
	Freshly ground pepper	
1 teaspoon	chopped fresh tarragon OR ½ teaspoon (2 mL) dried tarragon	5 mL
1	leek	1
1 tablespoon	unsalted butter	15 mL
1 teaspoon	finely chopped onion	5 mL
¼ cup	water	50 mL
½ cup	heavy (35%) cream	125 mL
1 tablespoon	Canadian port	15 mL
¼ cup	dry white wine	50 mL

1. Preheat oven to 400°F (200°C). Cut sorrel or spinach leaves into thick julienne strips.
2. In a saucepan, bring 6 cups of salted water to boil. Blanch sorrel for 30 seconds. Drain and rinse under cold running water to set colour. Drain and set aside.
3. Flatten fish fillets slightly by pressing them down gently with side of cleaver; sprinkle with salt, pepper, and tarragon.
4. Divide drained sorrel into six bundles. Flatten a bundle on top of each fillet. Roll each fillet up, starting at widest end, rolling toward the pointier end (if there is one). Secure each rolled-up fillet with 2 toothpicks–one at each end of roll.
5. Cut each rolled-up fillet in half crosswise through the centre point; this will give two rolls, each secured by a toothpick.
6. Trim and discard bottoms and greens of leek; split white portion lengthwise, wash carefully, and cut into julienne strips.
7. Butter a small, flame-proof baking pan and sprinkle evenly with onion and leek. Place fillets on top, either flat end down.
8. In a bowl, mix together water, cream, port, and wine. Pour over fillets.
9. Place baking pan over medium heat, and bring liquid to boil. Remove from heat, cover with greased waxed or parchment paper. Bake for 7 minutes.
10. Remove fillet rolls, placing end down on paper towels to drain. Reduce sauce in baking dish over high heat until thick enough to coat a wooden spoon.
11. Pour sauce onto serving dish and arrange fillets, end up, in sauce. Serve hot.

LAKE ONTARIO SMELTS, HOME-STYLE

This recipe calls for sorrel, which has a distinctive, soury taste. The hearty sorrel plant is a perennial that grows in most of Canada.

In many recipes, you can substitute spinach for sorrel; in this one, however, use fresh parsley.

Serves 2.

8	smelts, preferably fresh	8
3 tablespoons	flour	45 mL
1/2 teaspoon	salt	2 mL
1/8 teaspoon	freshly ground pepper	0.5 mL
1/2 cup	milk	125 mL
1/2 cup	vegetable oil	125 mL

SAUCE:		
2 teaspoons	unsalted butter	10 mL
1 tablespoon	finely chopped onion	15 mL
1 tablespoon	flour	15 mL
1/4 cup	dry white wine	50 mL
3/4 cup	cold water	175 mL
1	bay leaf	1
2 tablespoons	finely chopped sorrel OR fresh parsley	30 mL
1	clove garlic, finely chopped	1
2 teaspoons	soy sauce	10 mL

1. Wash smelts thoroughly under cold running water. Remove heads and discard.
2. In a bowl, mix together flour, salt, and pepper. Dip smelts in milk, and then dredge lightly with flour mixture.
3. In a frying pan, heat oil over medium heat. Fry smelts until golden, about 1 to 1 1/2 minutes on each side.
4. Transfer smelts to a serving dish and keep warm until serving.
5. Drain excess fat from pan and discard. Using the same pan to make sauce (this augments flavour) add butter. Over medium heat, lightly sauté onion.
6. Add flour and continue stirring for about 1 minute. Do not permit flour to stick or burn.
7. In a separate bowl, mix all remaining ingredients. Add to frying pan.
8. Cook slowly over medium heat until mixture thickens and is reduced to half. Season to taste. Pour into sauceboat and serve with smelts.

QUEEN CRAB IN
YOGURT WITH GINGER

Rather than Alaska king crab, which is not a product of our coasts, we have chosen queen crab, which inhabits our Maritime waters. Cooked, frozen queen crab comes in 1-pound (450-g) packages containing body and leg meat.

This recipe calls for crystallized ginger. See our recipe on page 222.

This dish goes nicely with Lemon and Parsley Rice (page 185) or new boiled potatoes.

Serves 2.

1 tablespoon	unsalted butter	15 mL
1 tablespoon	finely chopped onion	15 mL
6	firm white mushroom caps, sliced, not too thin	6
1 teaspoon	curry powder	5 mL
1½ teaspoons	crystallized ginger, very finely chopped(page 222)	7 mL
2 tablespoons	Canadian sherry	30 mL
1 cup	plain yogurt (*not* skim-milk variety)	250 mL
1 teaspoon	Worcestershire sauce	5 mL
½ teaspoon	salt	2 mL
½ pound	queen crab meat (from body and legs), cut in pieces about ½ inch (1.5 cm) long	225 g

1. Melt butter in a sauté pan over medium heat. When foam subsides, sauté onion until soft and transparent.
2. Add mushrooms and sauté 1 additional minute. Increase heat to high and cook 1 additional minute.
3. Add curry and ginger, stirring constantly, and cook 1 additional minute.
4. Reduce heat to medium. Add sherry to deglaze pan. Reduce liquid to half.
5. Add yogurt and Worcestershire sauce. Reduce liquid again to half.
6. Add salt. Add crab and cook until meat is heated through. Serve at once.

CHILLED FILLETS OF RAINBOW TROUT WITH DILL SAUCE

An original creation for The Best of Canada, this dish was inspired by Sweden's gravlax. Our dish features four raw trout fillets cured in a herbed wine marinade.

The dish tastes best when made 2 days in advance of serving.

Serves 2 as an entrée, 4 as an appetizer.

2	fresh rainbow trout	2

MARINADE:

1 cup	cold water	250 mL
1½ teaspoons	Dijon mustard	7 mL
¼ cup	cider vinegar	50 mL
½ cup	dry white wine	125 mL
½ teaspoon	finely chopped tarragon	2 mL
½ teaspoon	black peppercorns	2 mL
1	bay leaf	1
8	slices of carrot, each ¼ inch (0.75 cm) thick	8
1	clove garlic, crushed	1
2	thin slices of purple onion	2
1 teaspoon	salt	5 mL

SAUCE:

½ cup	sour cream	125 mL
1 teaspoon	horseradish	5 mL
2 teaspoons	finely chopped fresh dill	10 mL
1 tablespoon	dry sherry	15 mL

GARNISH:

4	sprigs fresh dill	4
1	lime, quartered lengthwise	1

1. Rinse fish under cold running water and pat dry with paper towels. Discard head and tail, and fillet each fish into 2 pieces. Set aside.
2. To make marinade, mix together all ingredients in a stainless-steel or enamel saucepan (aluminium will turn fish black) over high heat. Bring mixture to boil, stirring, and cook for 3 minutes.
3. Meanwhile, arrange fillets in a flat glass or porcelain dish, skin side up. Cover with hot marinade and let cool before refrigerating. For best taste, refrigerate, covered, 2 days.
4. To serve, remove fillets from marinade. Peel off skin and scrape out greyish-black line of fat that runs lengthwise down centre of each fillet just under skin. (This fat tastes a bit like cod-liver oil and alters taste of dill sauce). Arrange fillets on serving dish and garnish with carrots and purple onion from marinade.
5. To make sauce, mix together all ingredients and chill. Garnish each fillet with sprig of fresh dill and a lime wedge. Serve with sauce.

MEATS

Serves 6.

1	**3-pound (1.3-kg) rump roast**	1
2	**onions, sliced**	2
2	**carrots, sliced**	2
8	**whole peppercorns**	8
1	**bay leaf**	1
½ teaspoon	**thyme**	2 mL
4	**sprigs parsley**	4
1⅔ cups	**dry red wine**	400 mL
2 tablespoons	**unsalted butter**	30 mL
2 teaspoons	**oil**	10 mL
24	**fresh (*not* pickled) pearl onions, peeled**	24
16	**mushroom caps**	16
4	**cloves garlic, peeled**	4
1 tablespoon	**flour**	15 mL
8	**slices bacon, cut into julienne strips**	8
	Salt and freshly ground pepper	
6	**slices white bread**	6
2 tablespoons	**Canadian brandy**	30 mL

1. Cut roast into 2-inch (5-cm) cubes.
2. In a bowl, combine beef, onions, carrots, peppercorns, bay leaf, thyme, parsley, and dry red wine. Let sit, refrigerated, at least 24 hours. Turn cubes of meat every few hours to maximize flavour absorption.
3. In a flame-proof casserole or large saucepan, melt butter and oil over medium heat. (The addition of oil reduces likelihood of burning.) Sauté pearl onions until golden, turning constantly. Remove and set aside.
4. Sauté mushrooms, stirring constantly, until lightly browned. Remove and set aside.
5. Add whole garlic cloves to pan. Remove meat from marinade and pat cubes dry with paper towels. Reserve marinade.
6. Dust meat lightly with flour and add to pan, a few pieces at a time. Brown meat, setting pieces aside when done. Add additional cubes of beef until all are cooked. Set beef aside. Drain excess fat from casserole. Discard garlic.

7. Meanwhile, in a separate saucepan over high heat, bring marinade to boil. Reduce liquid to half and strain through fine sieve.
8. Pour strained liquid into casserole. Add cubes of beef, sautéed pearl onions, mushrooms, and bacon. Salt and pepper to taste. Bring to boil, reduce heat, and simmer, covered, 1½ to 2 hours.
9. To make croutons, remove the crusts from bread slices. Cut each slice into shape of a heart and lightly toast.
10. When beef is tender, transfer with vegetables to serving platter and keep warm. Reserve liquid in casserole; add brandy and bring sauce to boil. Strain through fine sieve and serve with meat.
11. Decorate each serving with 1 crouton. As well, small new potatoes or *pommes parisiennes* are suitable accompaniments.

BRAISED BEEF WITH HERBS AND HAZELNUTS

Here's a happy herb and hazelnut creation that we developed after several trials. By simmering slowly, the meat cooks in its own juices. There should be enough liquid remaining after braising to serve as gravy.
    Serves 6.

1	medium-sized carrot	1
1	whole bud (bulb) garlic, unpeeled	1
1 tablespoon	oil, preferably hazelnut	15 mL
2	bay leaves	2
½ teaspoon	whole black peppercorns	2 mL
6	small fresh (not pickled) pearl onions OR ½ small onion, coarsely chopped	6
2	small, ripe tomatoes, whole and unpeeled	2
½ teaspoon	thyme	2 mL
1	3½-pound (1.5-kg) lean blade roast cut into 2-inch (5-cm) cubes	1
1 teaspoon	salt	5 mL
¼ cup	dry white wine	50 mL
¼ cup	dry sherry	50 mL
¼ cup	hazelnuts, shelled but still in brown skins	50 mL
2 tablespoons	finely chopped parsley	30 mL

1. Cut carrot into thick slices. Cut unpeeled garlic bud in half crosswise.
2. In a saucepan, heat oil over medium heat. Add bay leaves, peppercorns, carrot, garlic, and onions and sauté until onions are lightly browned.
3. Add tomatoes, thyme, and beef cubes. Sprinkle with salt. Increase heat to high and sear meat, stirring constantly. Do not brown meat through; cook about 5 minutes.
4. Add wine and sherry. Bring to boil, reduce heat and simmer, covered, 1 1/2 to 1 3/4 hours.
5. Meanwhile toast hazelnuts in 375°F (190°C) oven for 5 minutes. Chop toasted nuts coarsely.
6. About 10 minutes before meat is done, stir in hazelnuts. Cover and finish cooking.
7. Transfer beef to serving dish. Discard garlic bud. Pour pan juices over beef. Sprinkle with parsley.
8. Serve with Gingered Carrots (page 155) or boiled new potatoes.

LONDON BROIL FLANK STEAK

The London Broil is a tasty dish that makes use of a some-times tough cut of beef, the flank. The secret of tenderizing a flank steak lies in the marinade; ours tastes great and works wonders.

As an option to broiling the steak, we've presented tips on how to sauté, an unusual treatment for this cut of beef.

If broiling, one way to keep your steak from getting tough is to keep it rare; the longer a flank steak is broiled, the tougher it becomes.

Serves 6 to 8.

1	**3-pound (1.3-kg) flank steak**	1

MARINADE:

¹/₂ teaspoon	**dry mustard**	2 mL
¹/₂ cup	**wine vinegar**	125 mL
¹/₂ cup	**cold water**	125 mL
1 cup	**olive oil**	250 mL
1 teaspoon	**coarsely crushed peppercorns**	5 mL
1 tablespoon	**mixed pickling spices**	15 mL
1 teaspoon	**salt**	5 mL
2	**cloves garlic, crushed**	2

1. In a large bowl, combine all ingredients of marinade. Add steak and marinate, refrigerated, for 2 to 5 days. Turn steak daily.
2. About 5 minutes prior to cooking, remove steak from marinade. Drain and pat lightly with paper towel.
3. To broil: preheat broiler. Place steak on rack with a drip pan. Steak should be about 1 ¹/₂ inches (4 cm) beneath broiling element. Broil 4 to 5 minutes per side, turning only once. Cook medium rare to maximize tenderness.
4. To serve, cut thin slices against the grain.
5. **Optionally**, sauté meat: cut steak into ¹/₄-inch (1-cm) thick slices (against grain) before cooking. In a sauté pan over medium heat, melt ¹/₄ cup (50 mL) unsalted butter. When foam subsides, sauté flank strips. Season with salt and cook for about 1 minute each side. Serve at once on slice of toasted rye bread. Garnish with dill pickles.

CANADIAN ROAST
RIB OF BEEF *AU JUS*

Serves 4.

1	clove garlic	1
1	2-pound (900-g) standing rib roast	1
1 teaspoon	crushed OR coarsely ground pepper	5 mL
1 tablespoon	salt	15 mL
1 tablespoon	dry mustard	15 mL
4	medium-sized baking potatoes	4
1	onion	1
1	carrot	1
1 tablespoon	oil	15 mL
1	bay leaf	1

GRAVY:

1 ½ cups	water	375 mL
1 teaspoon	cornstarch dissolved in ½ cup (125 mL) water	5 mL
	Salt and freshly ground pepper	
1	beef bouillon cube (optional)	1

1. Cut garlic clove into 5 slices diagonally. Insert 5 garlic slices into crown of roast. (In 5 different places along crown, insert a knife tip about 1 inch [2.5 cm] into beef. While blade is inserted, slide a sliver of garlic down knife face into beef. Pull blade out, leaving garlic buried in beef.)
2. Rub exterior of beef with pepper, salt, and mustard. Set beef aside for 1 hour.
3. Preheat oven to 400°F (200°C).
4. While meat is absorbing spices, cut unpeeled potatoes in half, cut unpeeled onion in half, slice carrot into ½-inch (1.5-cm) pieces.
5. Heat oil in roasting pan in oven. When oil is sizzling hot, add potatoes, face down in oil. Add onion, face down, carrot slices, and bay leaf.
6. Cover with beef. Roast 1 hour, basting every 15 minutes. Remove potatoes and keep warm. Cook beef for additional 15 minutes or until done. (For rare meat, cook 20 minutes at 400°F [200°C] and an additional 35 minutes at 300°F [150°C]).

7. Transfer beef to serving platter and keep warm. Drain excess oil from pan.
8. To make gravy, add water to roasting pan and, over medium heat, reduce liquid to half.
9. Add dissolved cornstarch mixture. Bring to boil and cook, stirring, about 1 minute. Season to taste. (Optional: add 1 beef bouillon cube to heighten flavour.) Strain sauce. Transfer to sauceboat and serve with roast beef and potatoes.

1929 HAMBURGER

Why is this the 1929 hamburger? I asked Tony if it was because the lean ground chuck he was using was marked down from $19.30 – which is probably what we'll be paying per pound before long. "No, it's like a hamburger we used to make during the Depression – using a little of this and a little of that to mix with the meat," said Tony.

The budget-wise cook can throw these burgers together in minutes and the only bread lines forming will be family members grabbing buns, lining up for seconds.

While any soy sauce will do, we prefer the lighter coloured, lighter flavoured Japanese brands. These burgers are also excellent broiled, and even better barbecued on a hot summer's eve.

Yield: 4 burgers.

1 pound	lean ground chuck	450 g
1 teaspoon	salt	5 mL
1 teaspoon	powdered chicken stock	5 mL
2 tablespoons	ketchup	30 mL
1 teaspoon	soy sauce	5 mL
¼ teaspoon	freshly ground pepper	1 mL
¼ teaspoon	Worcestershire sauce	1 mL
¼ cup	coarsely chopped onion	50 mL
2 tablespoons	oil, for frying	30 mL

1. Mix together all ingredients, except oil. Shape into patties.
2. In a heavy frying pan, heat oil over medium heat. Pan-fry patties until done as desired.

METRO MEATBALLS

Despite the long list of ingredients, this is an easy dish to assemble. Great for entertaining, as the meatballs can be made in advance and reheated for party use.

The meatballs may be cooked in the sauce that follows, or in the pepper and tomato sauce for Picnic Chicken (page 122).

Yield: 35 meatballs.

MEATBALLS:

¾ cup	crumbled stale white bread	175 mL
½ cup	hot milk	125 mL
5	slices bacon, cut into small pieces	5
½ cup	finely chopped onion	125 mL
1½ pounds	lean ground beef	675 g
2	cloves garlic, finely chopped	2
2 tablespoons	finely chopped parsley	30 mL
1 tablespoon	paprika	15 mL
1 teaspoon	thyme	5 mL
1 teaspoon	ground cumin	5 mL
1 teaspoon	Worcestershire sauce	5 mL
1	small egg, beaten	1
1½ teaspoons	salt	7 mL
½ teaspoon	freshly ground pepper	2 mL
2 teaspoons	powdered chicken stock	10 mL
2 tablespoons	oil, for cooking	30 mL

SAUCE:

1 tablespoon	oil	15 mL
1	large onion, finely chopped	1
1	large tomato, peeled, seeded, chopped	1
1	bay leaf	1
1	10-ounce (285-g) bag spinach, washed, stems removed	1
4	medium-sized carrots, peeled, cut into 1-inch (2.5-cm) pieces	4
1 teaspoon	thyme	5 mL
2	cloves garlic, crushed	2
3	medium-sized potatoes, peeled and quartered	3
	Salt and freshly ground pepper	
4 cups	water	1 L

1. To make meatballs, soak bread in hot milk for about 5 minutes.
2. Lightly sauté bacon in a sauté pan over medium heat. Add onion and sauté until soft.
3. Mix soaked bread, bacon, and onions with remaining ingredients, excluding oil. Mix thoroughly with hands. Shape into small, golf-ball-sized balls.
4. In a frying pan, heat oil over medium heat. Sauté meatballs until entirely brown.
5. To make sauce, heat oil in a large saucepan over medium heat. Add onion and sauté until transparent.
6. Add tomato and sauté 3 additional minutes. Add bay leaf, spinach, carrots, thyme, garlic, and potatoes. Add salt and pepper to taste. Add water. Bring to boil, reduce heat, and simmer, uncovered, 20 minutes.
7. Add meatballs and simmer, covered, 20 additional minutes.

MIGHTY MIDWEEK MEAT LOAF

Here's a delicious meat loaf to make on Sunday and serve hot; count on making sandwiches early in the week and reheat what's left for Wednesday's dinner.

It's one of those dishes that gets better with thyme.

Serves 6.

3	slices whole-wheat OR white bread	3
⅔ cup	warm milk	150 mL
1 tablespoon	oil	15 mL
2 tablespoons	finely chopped onion	30 mL
1	egg, beaten	1
2	cloves garlic, finely chopped	2
1 tablespoon	finely chopped parsley	15 mL
3 tablespoons	ketchup	45 mL
1 tablespoon	powdered chicken stock	15 mL
1 tablespoon	soy sauce	15 mL
¾ teaspoon	salt	4 mL
2 teaspoons	thyme	10 mL
2 teaspoons	Worcestershire sauce	10 mL
¾ teaspoon	freshly ground pepper	4 mL
1 cup	finely chopped ham	250 mL
½ cup	finely chopped celery	125 mL
2 pounds	medium-lean ground chuck	900 g
	Bread crumbs	
1	bay leaf	1

1. Preheat oven to 375°F (190°C).
2. Cut crust from bread and discard. (The crust is slightly burned, and may impart an undesirable flavour to the meat loaf. Moreover, the crust doesn't soak up liquid as easily as the soft interior of the loaf does.)
3. Soak bread in warm milk. Let stand 15 minutes.
4. Meanwhile, heat oil in a sauté pan over medium heat. Sauté onion until soft.
5. In a large bowl, combine soaked bread, egg, sautéed onion, garlic, parsley, ketchup, powdered chicken stock, soy sauce, salt, thyme, Worcestershire sauce, and pepper. Mix well.
6. Add ham, celery, and ground beef. Thoroughly blend.
7. Shape meat into loaf and roll lightly in bread crumbs before placing in a well-greased loaf pan or baking dish. Decorate top with bay leaf. Bake 50 to 60 minutes or until done.

ALBERTA SIRLOIN STEAK
WITH BLACK PEPPER SAUCE

The secret to make the dish zing is to use coarsely ground black peppercorns. Coarsely ground pepper gives a much different flavour to foods than finely milled, dust-like pepper.

Serves 2.

2	8-ounce (225-g) sirloin steaks (strip loin or filet)	2
1 teaspoon	coarsely ground pepper	5 mL
¼ teaspoon	salt	1 mL
2 tablespoons	unsalted butter	30 mL
1 tablespoon	finely chopped shallots OR onion	15 mL
½ cup	dry red wine	125 mL
1 tablespoon	Canadian brandy	15 mL
½ cup	heavy (35%) cream	125 mL
	Salt and pepper to taste	
½ teaspoon	beef extract (optional)	2 mL
1 teaspoon	finely chopped parsley	5 mL

1. Sprinkle both sides of steaks with pepper and salt.
2. In a heavy frying pan over medium heat, melt butter. When foam subsides, increase heat to high, add steaks and quickly sauté until browned on both sides. Reduce heat to medium and fry about 7 additional minutes. Transfer steaks to warmed dish, and set aside.
3. Drain half the fat and sauté shallots until soft and transparent.
4. Add wine and reduce liquid to half.
5. Add brandy, cream, and any juices accumulated in steak dish. Reduce liquid to half again. Salt and pepper to taste.
6. Add beef extract. (This is optional. The extract gives sauce more zip, but you'll still have a marvellously rich sauce without it.)
7. Pour sauce over steaks. Sprinkle with chopped parsley and serve at once.

POT-AU-FEU MOOSE JAW

Pot-au-feu *is a classical French 2-in-1 dish, comprising boiled beef and a clear consommé in which the beef has been boiled.*

In the late sixties, Tony served this dish to broadcaster Gordon Sinclair at the Westbury in Toronto. Gordon used to say it was "the best beef stew in the world – after my wife's." Strong praise from crusty old Gordon.

We've named this dish after Saskatchewan's friendliest city. Not so much because the people are hospitable – which they are – but because we've also tested this beef recipe using moose. We substituted a 4-pound (1.8-kg) moose shoulder blade roast for the short rib roast, and had a tender, tasty mouthful of moose and didn't even have to strain our jaw.

Serves 4.

4	carrots	4
2	white turnips	2
2	large leeks	2
½	medium-sized cabbage	½
2	onions, only *one* peeled	2
1	marrow bone	1
1	4-pound (1.8-kg) roast (short rib, rump, or blade)	1
16 cups	cold water	4 L
1	bay leaf	1
½ teaspoon	black peppercorns	2 mL
4	new potatoes, peeled	4
	Salt and freshly ground pepper	
	Chopped parsley to decorate	

1. Peel carrots and cut into 1½-inch (4-cm) pieces.
2. Cut and discard turnip tops. Peel and halve turnips lengthwise. Cut halves into pieces 1 ½ inches (4 cm) long.
3. Using white and light green portion of leeks, cut each lengthwise to within ½ inch (1.5 cm) of bulb bottom; spread leaves and wash thoroughly under running water. Bind each leek with string and set aside.
4. Wash cabbage half (cut lengthwise) without separating leaves; bind with string.
5. Cut unpeeled onion in half crosswise and place cut-side up under broiler until deeply browned. (This will give colour and taste to soup stock.)
6. Place carrots, turnips, leeks, cabbage, *whole peeled* onion, and marrow bone in a large saucepan filled with 8 cups (2 L) cold water. Bring to boil, add roast, and cook 1 minute. Drain and rinse ingredients under cold running water.
7. Return ingredients to saucepan. Cover with 8 cups (2 L) fresh cold water. Add browned onion halves, bay leaf, peppercorns, and potatoes. Bring to boil, reduce heat and simmer, uncovered, 12 to 15 minutes, or until vegetables are tender but still crisp. Skim surface periodically to remove fat. Remove all vegetables except burned onion halves; set aside and keep vegetables warm.
8. Continue cooking beef, marrow bone, and browned onion halves until meat is tender, about 1½ hours. Skim fat off surface periodically.
9. Discard onion halves and bay leaf. Remove string from vegetables. Serve consommé and then beef with vegetables. Or serve together in soup bowls. Salt and pepper to taste before serving and garnish each bowl with chopped parsley.

SIRLOIN STEAK À LA RICHE CHASSEUR

Classically, a dish made à la chasseur is one prepared with sautéed mushrooms, shallots, and white wine. But as this is a Canadian dish, and since classic food rules were made – like eggs – to be broken so that they might be enjoyed, we've designed our own steak à la chasseur.

The "rich" in the title has more to do with the oozy, sensual goodness of the sauce than it does with the wealth required to buy the ingredients.

Serves 4.

4	8-ounce (225-g) sirloin steaks	4
	Salt and freshly ground pepper	
1 tablespoon	unsalted butter	15 mL
1 tablespoon	finely chopped onion	15 mL
1	tomato, peeled, seeded, diced	1
8	mushroom caps, thinly sliced	8
1	clove garlic, finely chopped	1
½ teaspoon	tarragon	2 mL
½ teaspoon	chopped fresh parsley	2 mL
½ cup	dry red wine	125 mL
2 tablespoons	heavy (35%) cream	30 mL
½	beef bouillon cube	½

1. Season steaks with salt and pepper.
2. In a sauté pan over medium heat, melt butter. When foam subsides, increase heat to high and sauté steaks on both sides until browned. Do not cook through.
3. Reduce heat to medium and continue to sauté 1 additional minute. Remove steaks and keep warm.
4. Pour off half the fat. Add onion to pan and sauté until transparent, about 30 seconds. Add diced tomato and cook 1 additional minute.
5. Add mushrooms and garlic. Cook 1 additional minute.
6. Add tarragon, parsley, and red wine. Reduce liquid to half.
7. Add cream and beef cube, stirring until cube dissolves. Reduce liquid until thick enough to coat wooden spoon.
8. Add accumulated juice from steaks. Salt and pepper to taste.
9. To serve fashionably, pour sauce on plate first and cover with steak. Serve at once.

NORTHERN ONTARIO RABBIT
WITH FRESH GARDEN HERBS

For too many Canadians, the closest they've ever come to rabbit is Welsh rarebit, which isn't even the four-footed kind.

Rabbit is one of the leanest meats. It is the basis for some of Europe's finest, and tastiest, dishes. Cooking is simple; it may be treated exactly like chicken, to which many relate its taste, colour, and texture.

Italian, Portuguese, and Greek families make rabbit a part of their regular meal plans, and you will find fresh rabbit in many of their neighbourhood markets. It is now also available in many supermarkets.

Butchers will cut, or sometimes bone, a rabbit for customers. For most recipes, treat rabbit as you would chicken, cutting it into six pieces. Our recipe calls for a rabbit cut into 26 pieces: the two back legs cut into 3 pieces each, the forelegs cut into 2 pieces each, and the back split lengthwise, each half cut into 8 pieces.

Serves 6.

MARINADE:

	Juice of ½ lemon	
½ cup	dry sherry	125 mL
1½ teaspoons	Worcestershire sauce	7 mL
1	clove garlic, finely chopped	1
1	bay leaf	1
2 tablespoons	fresh OR 2 teaspoons (10 mL) dried chervil	30 mL
1 tablespoon	finely chopped mint	15 mL
1 tablespoon	Dijon mustard	15 mL
1 teaspoon	thyme	5 mL
1 teaspoon	rosemary	5 mL
½ teaspoon	tarragon	2 mL
¼ teaspoon	freshly ground pepper	1 mL
¼ teaspoon	sage	1 mL
1	3½-pound (1.5-kg) rabbit, cut into 26 pieces (method described above)	1
6 tablespoons	olive oil	90 mL
	Salt	
½ cup	chopped walnuts	125 mL
2 tablespoons	finely chopped parsley	30 mL

1. To make marinade, combine all ingredients in a bowl. Add rabbit. Cover and refrigerate at least 24 hours.
2. To cook, preheat oven to 375°F (190°C). Remove rabbit pieces from marinade and pat dry. Reserve marinade.
3. In a large saucepan, heat oil over medium heat. Fry rabbit pieces, turning frequently, until brown on all sides. Transfer to ovenproof casserole. Sprinkle lightly with salt. Cover with marinade. Sprinkle with walnuts.
4. Bake 1 hour.
5. Sprinkle with parsley and serve.

LAMB CHOPS JANUARY FOURTH

In foreign capitals, streets and public squares are frequently named after significant dates–birthdays of folk heroes, famous battles, and the like. We were working on this lamb recipe just after New Year's Day when Tony came up with a revolutionary touch: lemon and anchovies. To immortalize the culinary landmark, we've named the dish Lamb Chops January Fourth.
    Serves 2.

6	2-ounce (60-g) lamb chops	6
	Salt and freshly ground pepper	
2 tablespoons	unsalted butter	30 mL
¼ cup	sliced mushrooms	50 mL
1	tomato, peeled, seeded, diced	1
1	clove garlic, finely chopped	1
1 teaspoon	chopped fresh OR	5 mL
	¼ teaspoon (1 mL) dried tarragon	
⅛ teaspoon	thyme	0.5 mL
¼ cup	dry sherry	50 mL
1 tablespoon	chopped fresh mint	15 mL
6	slices lemon, rind removed	6
6	anchovies	6

1. Season lamb chops with salt and pepper.
2. In a sauté pan over medium heat, melt butter. When foam subsides, sauté chops, about 4 to 5 minutes per side. The meat should brown on the outside but stay pink inside.
3. Transfer chops to a serving platter and keep warm. Drain excess fat from pan and add mushrooms, tomato, garlic, tarragon, and thyme and cook over medium heat about 4 minutes.
4. Add sherry and cook an additional 30 seconds. Pour sauce over lamb chops. Sprinkle with mint. Top each chop with a rindless slice of lemon and a rolled anchovy fillet. Serve at once.

HERBED LAMB CHOPS SAUTÉED

Shari Lewis wouldn't love this dish–Lambchop sautéed, indeed! But you will. It's created especially for The Best of Canada.
    Serves 2.

HERB MARINADE:

3 tablespoons	olive oil	45 mL
1	bay leaf, cut into pieces	1
½ teaspoon	thyme	2 mL
½	clove garlic, crushed	½
½ teaspoon	freshly ground pepper	2 mL
1 teaspoon	salt	5 mL
½ teaspoon	finely chopped mint	2 mL
½ teaspoon	oregano	2 mL
	Juice of ½ lemon	
6	2-ounce (60-g) lamb chops	6

2 tablespoons	unsalted butter	30 mL
2	tomatoes, peeled, seeded, cut into quarters	2
2 tablespoons	dry white wine	30 mL
½ teaspoon	oregano	2 mL
	Salt and freshly ground pepper	

1. Mix together marinade ingredients. Place lamb chops in marinade and refrigerate at least 2 hours.
2. Melt butter in a sauté pan over medium heat. When foam subsides, sauté chops, about 3 minutes each side. Chops should remain pink inside.
3. Remove chops and keep warm. Drain excess fat from pan; add tomatoes and sauté over medium heat about 1 minute.
4. Add white wine and oregano and cook additional 4 minutes. Salt and pepper to taste.
5. Pour sauce over chops and serve hot.

CANADIAN LEG OF SPRING LAMB WITH HERBS AND MUSTARD SEED

Serves 4.

1 tablespoon	salt	15 mL
½ teaspoon	freshly ground pepper	2 mL
½ teaspoon	thyme	2 mL
¼ teaspoon	oregano	1 mL
1 teaspoon	rosemary	5 mL
1	3½-pound (1.5-kg) leg of spring lamb	1
3 tablespoons	oil	45 mL
1	bay leaf	1
1	carrot, thinly sliced	1
1	small onion, quartered	1
1	clove	1
2 teaspoons	dry mustard	10 mL
¼ cup	milk	50 mL
¼ teaspoon	mustard seeds	1 mL
½ cup	fresh white bread crumbs	125 mL
2 tablespoons	chopped fresh parsley	30 mL
2	cloves garlic, finely chopped	2
¼ teaspoon	finely chopped mint	1 mL

1. Preheat oven to 350°F (180°C).
2. In a bowl, mix salt, pepper, thyme, oregano, and rosemary. Coat lamb with mixture.
3. In a roasting pan, heat oil over medium heat. When hot, add bay leaf, carrot, onion, and clove. Cook, stirring, about 1 minute. Cover vegetables with leg of lamb. Baste with pan oil before placing in oven.
4. Roast 60 minutes, basting about every 10 minutes. Remove from oven. Increase heat to 400°F (200°C).
5. Mix dry mustard with milk. Brush cooked lamb with the mixture, and sprinkle with mustard seed.
6. In a separate bowl, combine bread crumbs, parsley, garlic, and mint. Coat lamb with mixture, patting it on firmly. Return lamb to oven and roast additional 15 minutes, or until bread crumbs are brown and lamb is done. Allow lamb to sit 10 minutes before carving.

PORK HOCKS WITH
CABBAGE AND CARROTS

Pork hocks–some call them knuckles–are tasty and relatively inexpensive cuts of pork. In fact, these are the joints between the foot and lower leg (both front and back). They're usually 6 to 7 inches (15 to 18 cm) in length and are easier to handle if split in half, crosswise. Pork hocks have a succulent, gelatinous quality that is much prized in soups and stews.

Tony created this casserole at the height of summer using fresh juniper berries, but you'll find dried berries year-round in small packets in specialty shops. Dried berries work just fine.

Serves 4.

4	pork hocks, cut in half	4
5 cups	shredded cabbage	1.2 L
6	slices bacon, cut into pieces	6
1	large onion, finely chopped	1
1	bay leaf	1
6	juniper berries	6
1 teaspoon	thyme	5 mL
2	apples, peeled, quartered, sliced	2
1½ teaspoons	salt	7 mL
½ teaspoon	freshly ground pepper	2 mL
¾ cup	dry white wine	175 mL
½ cup	water	125 mL
6	medium-sized carrots, sliced	6

1. In a large pot, cover pork with water. Bring to boil and blanch 2 minutes. Drain and rinse pork under cold running water. Drain and set aside.
2. In same pot, cover cabbage with water. Bring to boil and blanch 2 minutes. Drain and rinse cabbage under cold running water. Drain and set aside.
3. In a sauté pan over medium heat, sauté bacon until crisp. Add onion and sauté until transparent. Add bay leaf, juniper berries, thyme, blanched cabbage, apples, salt, and pepper. Stir well.
4. Add white wine and water and bring to boil.
5. Preheat oven to 350°F (180°C).

6. Transfer half the cabbage-juniper berry mixture to a well-greased ovenproof casserole. Spread mixture evenly to cover bottom. Cover with blanched pork hocks. Cover with carrots. Crown with remaining cabbage mixture.
7. Salt and pepper to taste. Bake, covered, 1½ hours, or until done. A meal by itself, or serve with boiled potatoes.

TWOFORKS HAM AND PEAR CASSEROLE

Twoforks is the name of a river in northern Saskatchewan. It also describes the way you'll attack this delicious dish, created especially for The Best of Canada.
Serves 4.

2 tablespoons	unsalted butter	30 mL
1 cup	finely chopped onion	250 mL
2 tablespoons	flour	30 mL
1 cup	dry red wine	250 mL
1 cup	chicken stock	250 mL
4	medium-sized carrots, cut into julienne sticks	4
1 teaspoon	salt	5 mL
	Freshly ground pepper	
1 tablespoon	soy sauce	15 mL
1 tablespoon	paprika	15 mL
1 pound	ham, cut into 1-inch (2.5-cm) cubes	450 g
1	pear, peeled, quartered, cored, sliced	1

1. Melt butter in a sauté pan over medium heat. When foam subsides, sauté onion until transparent.
2. Add flour, increase heat to high, and cook until flour is lightly browned. Stir constantly to avoid sticking or burning.
3. Add wine, chicken stock, carrots, salt, pepper, soy sauce, paprika, and ham. Bring to boil, reduce heat, and simmer, covered, 20 minutes or until carrots are tender.
4. Add pear and cook 10 additional minutes. Serve hot.

PORK CHOPS BARTLETT:
PORK WITH PEARS

Talk about pears: try our Pork Chops Bartlett with Potato and Turnip Casserole (page 149).

Serves 2.

MARINADE:

	Juice of ½ lemon	
½ teaspoon	freshly ground pepper	2 mL
½ teaspoon	thyme	2 mL
½ teaspoon	dry mustard	2 mL
2	cloves garlic, thinly sliced	2
⅛ teaspoon	dried tarragon	0.5 mL
½ teaspoon	salt	2 mL

4	loin pork chops	4
2 tablespoons	oil	30 mL
1 tablespoon	finely chopped onion	15 mL
¼ cup	dry white wine	50 mL
¼ teaspoon	dry mustard	1 mL
½ cup	heavy (35%) cream	125 mL
2	Bartlett pears, peeled, quartered, cored, cut into ¼-inch (1-cm) slices	2
1 tablespoon	raisins	15 mL
	Salt and freshly ground pepper	
2 tablespoons	grated Canadian Emmenthal cheese	30 mL

1. In a bowl, combine marinade ingredients. Place chops in a casserole and coat with marinade.
2. Marinate, refrigerated, at least 5 hours or overnight.
3. In a sauté pan, heat oil over medium heat. Sauté pork chops 5 minutes per side or until cooked through. Transfer to ovenproof casserole and keep warm.
4. Drain excess fat from pan; over medium heat, sauté onion until transparent.
5. In a bowl, mix wine and mustard; add to onion and deglaze pan by reducing liquid to half.
6. Add cream, pear slices, and raisins, and simmer until liquid is again reduced to half. Season to taste.
7. Pour sauce over chops. Sprinkle with grated cheese and place under preheated broiler for 4 minutes or until golden.
8. Loosen belt by 2 notches and go to it.

PORK CHOPS BREADED
WITH WALNUTS

A special creation for The Best of Canada. *Serve with Best-Ever Broccoli (page 142), or with Cabbage Sautéed with Cumin (page 144).*
　　Serves 4.

MARINADE:

	Juice of ½ lemon	
2 tablespoons	soy sauce	30 mL
½ teaspoon	thyme	2 mL
1	bay leaf, cut into pieces	1
1	clove garlic, finely chopped	1
½ teaspoon	freshly ground pepper	2 mL
½ teaspoon	salt	2 mL
4	6-ounce (180-g) pork chops about ½ inch (1.5 cm) thick	4
2	eggs, beaten	2
2 tablespoons	milk	30 mL
¼ cup	ground walnuts	50 mL
¾ cup	bread crumbs	175 mL
¼ cup	flour	50 mL
2 tablespoons	unsalted butter	30 mL
1 tablespoon	oil	15 mL

1. Mix together marinade ingredients. Coat pork chops with marinade and let sit, refrigerated, at least 2 hours, or overnight.
2. In a bowl, beat eggs and milk.
3. In a separate bowl, mix together walnuts and bread crumbs.
4. Remove pork chops from marinade and pat dry with paper towels. Dredge with flour, dip in egg-milk mixture, and coat with walnut-bread crumb mixture.
5. In a sauté pan over medium heat, melt butter with oil. (The combination reduces chances of burning. If you prefer to cook only with butter, increase butter by 1 tablespoon [15 mL]).
6. When foam subsides, sauté pork chops, about 4 to 5 minutes per side. Serve at once.

PROVINCIAL PORK FILET

Nobody's quite sure whether the Provincial in the title refers to the lottery or a geographic boundary – a state of luck or a state of the nation? Whichever, we do know that this pork dish is good enough to serve to company. The finished meat is tender and mild as veal.

Serves 2 to 4.

2	8-ounce (225-g) pork filets (pork tenderloin)	2
3 tablespoons	oil	45 mL
2 teaspoons	dry mustard	10 mL
1 tablespoon	milk	15 mL
½ teaspoon	rosemary	2 mL
1	clove garlic, crushed	1
1 teaspoon	celery salt	5 mL
⅛ teaspoon	ground cloves	0.5 mL
1 teaspoon	salt	5 mL
½ teaspoon	freshly ground pepper	2 mL
½	onion, sliced	½
½	carrot, sliced	½
½	stalk celery, sliced	½
¼ cup	dry white wine	50 mL
½ cup	water	125 mL
1 teaspoon	cornstarch, with enough water to make paste	5 mL

1. Preheat oven to 400°F (200°C).
2. Brush filets with oil. In a bowl, mix together dry mustard and milk. Add rosemary, garlic, celery salt, cloves, salt, and pepper. Mix thoroughly and brush filets with mixture.
3. Place slices of onion, carrot, and celery in roasting pan. Cover with filets. Roast 60 minutes, or until done, basting about every 10 minutes. Turn filets once during hour.
4. Transfer pork to serving dish and keep warm. Drain excess fat from roasting pan; leave vegetables in pan. Add wine and reduce liquid to half over medium heat.
5. Add water, bring to boil, and boil for 3 minutes.
6. Add cornstarch paste, stir and cook an additional 30 seconds. (For thinner sauce, add more water.) Salt and pepper to taste.
7. Pour sauce over filets. Serve while hot.

ACORN SQUASH STUFFED
WITH ONTARIO PORK

Serves 2.

1	acorn squash	1
1 tablespoon	unsalted butter	15 mL
2	4-ounce (115-g) boneless pork chops, cut into 1-inch (2.5-cm) cubes	2
1/4 cup	finely chopped onion	50 mL
4	mushrooms, diced	4
1	medium-sized tomato, peeled, seeded, diced	1
1	clove garlic, finely chopped	1
1/2 teaspoon	thyme	2 mL
	Freshly ground pepper	
2 tablespoons	heavy (35%) cream	30 mL
2 tablespoons	dry white wine	30 mL
2 tablespoons	bread crumbs	30 mL
1/2 teaspoon	salt	2 mL

1. Preheat oven to 350°F (180°C).
2. Cut squash in half and remove seeds, being careful not to remove any pulp. Bake halves for 30 minutes.
3. Meanwhile, in a saucepan over medium heat, melt butter. When foam subsides, increase heat to high, and sauté pork cubes until brown.
4. Reduce heat to medium, add onion and mushrooms, and sauté additional 30 seconds.
5. Add tomato, garlic, thyme, and pepper, and sauté an additional 1 minute. Stir constantly.
6. Add cream, wine, bread crumbs, and salt. Stir well and remove pan from heat.
7. Remove squash from oven. Stuff and mound with pork mixture and return to oven. Bake additional 20 to 25 minutes or until squash is tender.
8. Before serving, place under broiler for 1 minute to give finished colour.

ROAST ONTARIO PORK STUFFED WITH GINGER AND COCONUT

This dish has a lot of ingredients, but it also has a lot going for it. We advise that you make the stuffing in advance for three reasons.

Convenience: an otherwise-harried host can take the stuffing from the refrigerator 2 hours before company arrives and finish this dish without having a kitchen full of pots to clean.

Cooking ease: it's much easier to stuff meat or poultry when the stuffing is cold or congealed. Warm stuffing tends to squoosh and ooze all over when you're working with it.

Safety: it's unwise to stuff meat or poultry with hot stuffing unless the dish is going into the oven pronto. Heated stuffings are fertile ground for bacteria, especially when they're in contact with meat or poultry waiting five or six hours to be cooked.

The ginger, coconut, and carrot stuffing is divine and works nicely for poultry, too.

Serves 4.

1	2½-pound (1.1-kg) pork loin	1

MARINADE:

1 tablespoon	dry mustard	15 mL
½ cup	Canadian port	125 mL
	Juice of 1 lemon	
½ cup	plain yogurt	125 mL
1 teaspoon	thyme	5 mL
2	cloves garlic, crushed	2
	Salt and freshly ground pepper	

STUFFING:

2 tablespoons	unsalted butter	30 mL
½	onion, finely chopped	½
¼ teaspoon	thyme	1 mL
	Freshly ground pepper	
1	medium-sized carrot, peeled, grated	1
⅔ cup	bread crumbs	150 mL
2 tablespoons	raisins	30 mL
2 tablespoons	grated coconut, fresh or dried	30 mL

1 teaspoon	crystallized ginger (page 222), finely chopped	5 mL
1 tablespoon	chopped fresh parsley	15 mL
1	egg, beaten	1
½ teaspoon	salt	2 mL
2 tablespoons	oil	30 mL

SAUCE:

1 cup	water	250 mL
½ cup	dry white wine	125 mL
1 teaspoon	cornstarch dissolved in ¼ cup (50 mL) warm water	5 mL

1. Ask butcher to prepare pork loin for stuffing. Or, to prepare the meat yourself: trim excess fat and cut loin off-centre lengthwise, cutting about ¾ way through roast. This will create a sort of hinged loin; by cutting off-centre you will have more of a flap than 2 equal hinged halves.
2. To make marinade, mix together dry mustard, port, and lemon juice. Add yogurt, thyme, and garlic. Mix well. Salt and pepper to taste.
3. Marinate loin at least 6 hours, refrigerated, turning at least once.
4. To make stuffing, melt butter in a sauté pan over medium heat. When foam subsides, sauté onion until transparent.
5. Add thyme, pepper, and carrot, and sauté an additional 3 minutes.
6. Add bread crumbs; stir for 30 seconds. Remove from heat; add raisins, coconut, ginger, parsley, egg, and salt. Mix well and let cool. Refrigerate for later use. Stuffing can be prepared in advance up to this point.
7. Preheat oven to 400°F (200°C).
8. Remove pork loin from marinade and pat dry with paper towels. Stuff marinated pork loin with cooled stuffing mixture just before roasting. Roll and secure with butcher's twine.
9. Heat 2 tablespoons (30 mL) oil in roasting pan in oven. When sizzling hot, add pork. Roast 60 to 80 minutes or until done. Baste every 15 minutes.
10. To make sauce, remove pork from roasting pan and set aside. Keep warm. Drain all but about 1 tablespoon (15 mL) fat from pan. Add water and wine to pan. Reduce liquid to half over medium heat.
11. Add dissolved cornstarch, stirring constantly, and bring sauce to a boil. Salt and pepper to taste. Strain and serve with pork.

MEDALLIONS OF CANADIAN MOOSE

Hunters know how tasty moose can be. Frequently, reporters and Toronto Star *staffers come into my test kitchen to ask how to cook the moose that Uncle Rick brought home last weekend. Until Tony created this superb dish, I never had anything to suggest.*

Serves 4.

12	2-ounce (60-g) moose filets OR loin chops, cut thin	12

MARINADE:		
1½ cups	dry red wine	375 mL
¼ cup	white vinegar	50 mL
2 teaspoons	whole black peppercorns	10 mL
1	bay leaf	1
	Small bunch of parsley	
	Pinch of thyme	
1	onion, diced in large cubes	1
1	medium-sized carrot, sliced	1
½	celeriac (celery root), peeled and diced OR ½ bunch celery, diced	½

2 tablespoons	unsalted butter	30 mL
1 cup	heavy (35%) cream	250 mL
2 tablespoons	Canadian brandy	30 mL

1. Place moose filets between sheets of waxed paper and pound thin. (If using loin chops, remove bone first.)
2. Place moose filets in a bowl or saucepan. Combine nine marinade ingredients and pour over meat. Cover and refrigerate for at least 2 days.
3. Remove moose from marinade and pat dry with paper towels. Reserve marinade.
4. Melt butter in a sauté pan over high heat. When butter browns, sauté filets, about 3 to 4 minutes per side. The interior should remain red. (If using loin chops, cook about 4 to 5 minutes per side.) Set pieces aside on a serving platter and keep warm.
5. Drain excess fat from pan; add marinade and, over high heat, reduce liquid to half. Strain through fine sieve and pour liquid into a clean saucepan.
6. Heat strained liquid over medium-high heat. Add cream and brandy and reduce sauce until thick enough to coat a wooden spoon. Season to taste. Pour over moose filets.

VEAL AND ZUCCHINI
WITH YOGURT

While you may enjoy skim-milk yogurt for breakfast, anything less than whole milk yogurt won't do for this recipe because the sauce will separate.

You may wish to substitute crème fraîche for the yogurt, especially if calories don't count. Make your own following our recipe (page 216). Substitute in equal volumes.

Serves 2.

12 ounces	veal loin, cut into 6 thin slices OR 6 veal cutlets	340 g
½ teaspoon	salt	2 mL
	Freshly ground pepper	
1 tablespoon	flour	15 mL
2 tablespoons	unsalted butter	30 mL
1 tablespoon	finely chopped shallots OR onion	15 mL
½	zucchini, thinly sliced	½
1	clove garlic, crushed	1
2 tablespoons	dry sherry	30 mL
1 cup	whole-milk yogurt	250 mL
1 teaspoon	chopped parsley	5 mL

1. Using a mallet or heavy saucepan, flatten veal to ¼-inch (1-cm) thickness between sheets of waxed paper or plastic wrap. Season both sides of veal with salt and pepper. Dredge with flour.
2. In a sauté pan over medium heat, melt butter. When foam subsides, sauté veal about 3 minutes per side or until lightly browned. Remove veal and keep warm. Sauté shallots in the pan until transparent.
3. Add zucchini and sauté an additional 1 to 2 minutes. Not more; zucchini must stay crisp. Add garlic and stir for an additional 15 seconds.
4. Add sherry and reduce liquid to half.
5. Add yogurt and reduce liquid to half again or until thick enough to coat wooden spoon. Salt and pepper to taste.
6. Place veal on serving dish. Cover with sauce and sprinkle with parsley. Serve with rice.

ESCALOPE OF VEAL
WITH BRANDY AND CREAM

The French say escalope, the Italians refer to a scaloppe, and the Canadians prefer scallop or veal cutlet . What they all mean is a thinly flattened piece of meat (usually veal, though sometimes turkey, chicken, or fish) that is fried in butter.

Here is a dandy treatment for veal with a rich brandy and cream sauce. Serve with buttered green noodles.
Serves 2.

12 ounces	veal loin, cut into 6 thin slices OR 6 veal cutlets	340 g
	Salt and freshly ground pepper	
2 tablespoons	flour	30 mL
¼ cup	unsalted butter	50 mL
1 tablespoon	finely chopped shallots OR onion	15 mL
4	mushroom caps, sliced	4
2 tablespoons	Canadian brandy	30 mL
¾ cup	heavy (35%) cream	175 mL

1. Flatten veal pieces to ¼-inch (1-cm) thickness between sheets of waxed paper or plastic wrap, using a meat mallet, heavy saucepan, or side of a large cleaver.
2. Sprinkle both sides of veal with salt and pepper. Dredge with flour.
3. Melt half the butter in a sauté pan over medium heat. When foam subsides, add veal and sauté lightly on both sides. Remove veal and keep warm. Add shallots and mushrooms to pan and cook for 1 minute.
4. Add brandy and cream and reduce liquid to half or until thick enough to coat a wooden spoon. Add any juices drained from veal.
5. Remove pan from heat and add remaining butter, a little at a time. Shake pan back and forth to help blend in butter. This gives a gloss to sauce. Season to taste, pour over veal, and serve immediately.

ESCALOPE DE VEAU
CANADIEN BLEU

Tony created this version of the classic, Veal Cordon Bleu, while chefing at the Westbury Hotel, Toronto.
Serves 2.

2	6-ounce (180-g) veal cutlets	2
4	slices Canadian Emmenthal cheese	4
2	slices ham	2
2	eggs	2
3 tablespoons	milk	45 mL
	Salt and freshly ground pepper	
2 tablespoons	flour	30 mL
	Bread crumbs	
2 tablespoons	unsalted butter	30 mL
4 tablespoons	grated old Cheddar cheese	60 mL

1. Preheat oven to 400°F (200°C).
2. Flatten cutlets between sheets of waxed paper to about ¼-inch (1-cm) thickness using mallet or bottom of heavy skillet.
3. Place 1 slice Emmenthal on each cutlet, covering just half the meat. Top each cheese slice with a single slice of ham. Cover ham with second slice of cheese. Fold veal, sandwiching layered ingredients. Crimp edges.
4. In a bowl, beat eggs and milk. Season mixture to taste with salt and pepper. Dredge folded cutlets with flour, coating both sides; dip in egg-milk mixture. Coat with bread crumbs.
5. In a sauté pan over medium heat, melt butter. When foam subsides, sauté cutlets until golden, about 3 minutes per side.
6. Transfer cutlets to baking dish. Bake 8 minutes.
7. Before serving, sprinkle each cutlet with 2 tablespoons (30 mL) grated Cheddar. Serve with Lemon and Parsley Rice, (page 185).

POULTRY

ROYALE DE CANARD CANADIEN: A FORCEMEAT OF DUCK WITH ORANGE SAUCE

Don't be put off by the fancy French name or the long list of ingredients. This is a ritzy way of saying "Duck Hamburgers with Gravy."

What we have created is a deliriously delicious plate of duck patties, made from a forcemeat of duck and bacon, that float in a heavenly stock seasoned with juniper berries and rosemary, sweetened with orange liqueur.

You will find dried juniper berries available year-round in gourmet and specialty shops, sold in small packets.

Serves 4 divinely.

FORCEMEAT:

1	4-pound (1.8-kg) duckling	1
3	slices bacon	3
1	egg white	1
½ teaspoon	salt	2 mL
	Freshly ground pepper	
2 tablespoons	coarsely chopped walnuts	30 mL
⅛ teaspoon	freshly grated nutmeg	0.5 mL
1 teaspoon	grated ginger root	5 mL
½ cup	heavy (35%) cream	125 mL

STOCK:

1 tablespoon	unsalted butter	15 mL
½ cup	chopped onion	125 mL
1	clove garlic, crushed	1
1 teaspoon	juniper berries, crushed	5 mL
½ teaspoon	black peppercorns	2 mL
1	small carrot, chopped	1
3	sprigs parsley	3
1	small tomato, chopped	1
½ teaspoon	finely chopped fresh OR dried rosemary	2 mL
1 teaspoon	tomato paste	5 mL
	Salt	
½ cup	dry white wine	125 mL
3 cups	water	750 mL

SAUCE:

1 tablespoon	buckwheat honey	15 mL
	Juice of 1 orange	

¼ cup	Melchers Kanata liqueur	50 mL
	Rind of 1 orange, cut into long, thin julienne strips, blanched in boiling water for 1 minute	
¼ cup	heavy (35%) cream	50 mL
1½ teaspoons	salt	7 mL
	Freshly ground pepper	
2 tablespoons	flour, sifted	30 mL
2 tablespoons	unsalted butter	30 mL

1. To prepare forcemeat of duck, skin and bone the duck, reserving duck bones for stock. Cut duck meat, duck liver, and bacon strips into small pieces. Place meat in food processor fitted with steel blade and purée. Transfer to stainless-steel bowl and refrigerate 30 minutes, or place in an enameled or china bowl and chill 2 hours. (The meat chills much more quickly in the stainless-steel bowl. You need a well-chilled forcemeat.)

2. When meat is sufficiently chilled, blend it thoroughly with egg white, salt, pepper, walnuts, nutmeg, and ginger. Using a wooden spoon, mix forcemeat and add cream in slow, steady trickle. Mix until cream is fully incorporated. Refrigerate at least 30 minutes before cooking.

3. To make stock, melt butter in a large saucepan over medium-high heat. Add onion, garlic, juniper berries, peppercorns, carrot, parsley, tomato, rosemary, and duck bones. Cook, stirring, until onion is lightly browned, about 15 minutes.

4. Add tomato paste; add salt to taste; add wine and water. Bring to boil, reduce heat, and simmer, uncovered, about 30 minutes or until stock is reduced to 1 cup (250 mL) liquid. Strain through fine sieve and set aside.

5. To make sauce, cook honey in a saucepan over high heat until honey turns a caramel colour. Add orange juice, Kanata liqueur, and strained duck stock. Reduce heat to medium and cook 2 minutes. Add half the julienne strips of orange rind and ¼ cup (50 mL) cream; cook 1 additional minute. Season with salt and pepper. Remove from heat but keep warm.

6. Shape duck forcemeat into 8 equal-sized patties – about 2 ounces (60 g) each. Dredge with flour.

7. In a sauté pan over medium heat, melt butter. When foam subsides, sauté patties about 5 minutes each side, or until golden in colour. Remove and set aside. Drain excess fat from pan; add duck sauce, return patties to pan, and simmer over medium heat, covered, 2 minutes.

8. To serve, arrange duck patties on a serving platter. Cover with sauce and sprinkle with remaining julienne strips of orange.
9. Serve with fresh buttered green beans and purée of celery root.

CHICKEN ROSEMARY

Contrary to what you may think, this dish was not named after a woman. In fact, it was created for Tony's own family. Whenever his kids clamour for chicken, this is what he cooks. The rosemary seasoning is superb. It has caught on in my home, too.

When cooked, the chicken should be crisp outside yet moist inside, due principally to the steaming wines. Don't expect a lot of residual sauce in the casserole, but what's left is finger lickin' fantastic.

Serves 4.

1	3-pound (1.3-kg) spring chicken	1
1 teaspoon	salt	5 mL
¼ cup	flour	50 mL
¼ cup	olive oil	50 mL
½ cup	dry Canadian sherry	125 mL
½ cup	dry white wine	125 mL
5 teaspoons	Dijon mustard	25 mL
¼ teaspoon	black peppercorns	1 mL
1 teaspoon	chopped fresh OR dried rosemary	5 mL
⅓ cup	coarsely chopped walnuts	75 mL
2	cloves garlic, coarsely chopped	2
3 tablespoons	coarsely chopped parsley	45 mL

1. Preheat oven to 375°F (190°C).
2. Split chicken in half lengthwise, and cut into pieces. Be sure to include liver and wings. Cut each leg into 2 pieces, each wing into 2 pieces, breast into 4 pieces, and liver into 4 pieces.
3. Season chicken pieces with salt and dredge in flour.
4. In a heavy frying pan, heat oil over high heat. The oil should be sizzling hot; this is what gives the chicken its golden-brownish colour.

5. Sauté chicken, turning occasionally, until browned. The outside will be cooked, but the interior of each piece will not be thoroughly done. Transfer pieces to ovenproof casserole.
6. Drain excess fat from frying pan; add sherry, white wine, and mustard to pan. Boil for about 1 minute to deglaze pan. Pour liquid over chicken.
7. Using the bottom of a saucepan, crush peppercorns. Sprinkle chicken with the coarsely ground pepper.
8. Sprinkle chicken with rosemary, walnuts, garlic, and parsley. Bake, uncovered, 25 to 30 minutes or until chicken is done. Serve hot.

CHICKEN LIVERS IN CREAM SAUCE

Serves 2.

1 tablespoon	unsalted butter	15 mL
12 ounces	chicken livers, fat removed, each liver cut into 4 pieces	340 g
$\frac{1}{2}$	large green pepper, finely chopped	$\frac{1}{2}$
$\frac{1}{8}$ teaspoon	thyme	0.5 mL
1 teaspoon	green peppercorns	5 mL
1	clove garlic, finely chopped	1
$\frac{1}{4}$ cup	dry sherry	50 mL
$\frac{1}{2}$ cup	heavy (35%) cream	125 mL
	Salt	
1 teaspoon	chopped chives	5 mL

1. Melt butter in a sauté pan over medium heat. When foam subsides, increase heat slightly and add liver. Sauté about 1 minute. Liver should be light brown outside, pink inside.
2. Remove liver and set aside. To juices in pan, add green pepper, thyme, green peppercorns, and garlic. Sauté over medium heat about 3 minutes
3. Add sherry to deglaze pan; reduce liquid to half.
4. Return liver pieces to pan; add cream. Cook about 2 minutes or until liver is heated through. Salt to taste.
5. Arrange liver on platter and cover with sauce. Sprinkle with chives and serve at once.

CAPE BRETON CONCOCTION: CHICKEN WITH MUSSELS

This dish doesn't know where it belongs, in the poultry part of the book or in the seafood section. We agree it belongs one place for sure: your tummy. It's delicious. It was created especially for The Best of Canada.

Serves 3 to 4.

1/2	2 1/2-pound (1-kg) chicken	1/2
1 teaspoon	salt	5 mL
	Freshly ground pepper	
2 tablespoons	flour	30 mL
2 tablespoons	unsalted butter	30 mL
1/2	onion, finely chopped	1/2
1	bay leaf	1
2	cloves garlic, finely chopped	2
1 tablespoon	chopped fresh coriander OR 1 teaspoon (5 mL) coriander seeds	15 mL
1/2 cup	dry white wine	125 mL
1 cup	chicken stock	1 L
1/2 cup	heavy (35%) cream	125 mL
30	mussels, scrubbed and debearded (see page 64)	30
	Pepper	
1 tablespoon	finely chopped parsley	15 mL

1. Cut chicken into serving pieces. Sprinkle with salt and pepper. Dredge with flour.
2. Melt butter in a sauté pan over medium heat. When foam subsides, sauté chicken until golden on both sides – about 3 minutes per side.
3. Remove chicken and set aside. Drain half the fat from pan. Add onion and bay leaf and sauté over medium heat until onion is soft and transparent, about 1 minute.
4. Reduce heat to low. Add garlic and *fresh* coriander and sauté lightly an additional 30 seconds. (If you are using coriander *seeds*: In a small pot, combine coriander seeds and white wine. Bring to boil for about 1 minute. Discard seeds and use coriander-scented wine in lieu of fresh coriander and the plain white wine.)
5. Return chicken to sauté pan. Add wine, or coriander-scented wine. Over high heat, reduce liquid to half.

6. Reduce heat to medium; add chicken stock and cook, covered, 20 to 25 minutes.
7. Add cream, then mussels, burying them in sauce. Cover and cook over high heat until all mussels open, about 5 minutes.
8. Pepper to taste. Place chicken and mussels on serving platter; cover with sauce and sprinkle with chopped parsley.

MARVELOUS MARINATED ROAST CHICKEN

Here's a way to spice up chicken. Make our zippy marinade in minutes, coat your chicken, and fire away! Makes family dinner special.
Serves 4.

1	small onion, finely chopped	1
1	clove garlic, finely chopped	1
1 teaspoon	paprika	5 mL
1 teaspoon	thyme	5 mL
1 teaspoon	salt	5 mL
4	drops Worcestershire sauce	4
	Freshly ground pepper	
1	bay leaf, cut into small pieces	1
	Fat of chicken cut from interior of cavity at tail end, finely chopped	
1 tablespoon	unsalted butter	15 mL
1	3-pound (1.3-kg) chicken	1

1. In a bowl, combine all ingredients except chicken.
2. Rub chicken, inside and out, with mixture. Let stand 1 hour before roasting.
3. Preheat oven to 375°F (190°C).
4. Roast chicken 40 minutes. Baste every 10 minutes with juices in pan. Remove from oven. Let stand 10 minutes before cutting.

SUNDAY GRILLED
SPRING CHICKEN

Tony created this dish for his family one Sunday afternoon and now it's caught on in both our homes for regular Sunday dinner. The secret is in the method of flattening the chicken. What you want is a sort of two-dimensional bird, flattened to resemble the pressed ducks that hang in barbecue huts in Chinatown.
   Serves 4.

1	3-pound (1.3-kg) chicken	1
2 tablespoons	unsalted butter, melted	30 mL
½ teaspoon	salt	2 mL
2 teaspoons	freshly ground pepper	10 mL
2 teaspoons	thyme	10 mL
1 teaspoon	paprika	5 mL
2 tablespoons	dry mustard	30 mL
2 tablespoons	buttermilk OR yogurt	30 mL
4	cloves garlic, finely chopped	4
1 tablespoon	chopped parsley	15 mL
2 tablespoons	fresh bread crumbs	30 mL

1. Preheat broiler and roasting pan.
2. To flatten chicken, use a cleaver to cut through backbone lengthwise, taking care not to cut through breast bone. Spread chicken out, hinging it on the uncut breast bone. Using back of cleaver, give a smart whack across the splayed breast. Then give each leg a whack at mid-joint. In each case, do not detach any part. What you want is a wholly joined but disjointed bird – one that can be flattened.
3. Brush chicken with melted butter. Combine salt, pepper, thyme, and paprika. Sprinkle chicken inside and out with seasoning mixture. (Most recipes call for a lot less pepper; ours is a peppery bird, so be generous with pepper.)
4. Transfer chicken to preheated roasting pan, breast-side up, and broil on middle rack 15 minutes.
5. Turn chicken over; broil an additional 15 minutes. Remove from oven and keep warm.
6. In a bowl, mix mustard and buttermilk. In a separate bowl, mix together garlic, parsley, and bread crumbs. Brush chicken skin with mustard paste. Sprinkle with garlic-bread crumb mixture. Return chicken to oven skin-side up; broil on middle rack until skin turns golden brown. Serve hot.

CHICKEN BREAST CORDON BLEU

A quick way to transform chicken breasts into something special.

Serves 2.

2	whole chicken breasts, boned and skinned	2
½ teaspoon	salt	2 mL
2	slices Canadian Cheddar cheese	2
1 teaspoon	chives	5 mL
2	slices ham	2
1 tablespoon	flour	15 mL
	Freshly ground pepper	
1	egg	1
2 tablespoons	milk	30 mL
3 tablespoons	fresh bread crumbs	45 mL
2 tablespoons	unsalted butter	30 mL

1. Preheat oven to 350°F (180°C).
2. Using a mallet, flatten breasts between sheets of waxed paper. (Each breast should be hinged in the middle but remain whole.)
3. Sprinkle chicken lightly with half the salt. Place 1 slice of cheese on underside of each breast, covering just half the breast. Sprinkle cheese with chives, then cover with slice of ham.
4. Fold breast in half, sandwiching cheese and ham; pinch edges.
5. In a bowl, mix together flour, remaining salt, and pepper. In a separate bowl, beat together egg and milk. Dredge chicken in flour. Dip with egg-milk mixture. Coat with fresh bread crumbs.
6. In a sauté pan over medium heat, melt butter. When foam subsides, sauté chicken until golden, about 2 to 3 minutes per side.
7. Transfer to ovenproof casserole. Bake, uncovered, 8 to 10 minutes. Serve hot.

PICNIC CHICKEN

This original chicken recipe calls for garden vegetables and herbs that many of us grow. However, you'll note that we prefer canned tomatoes to the fresh variety: canned tomatoes are in season 12 months of the year and have an identifiable tomato flavour. Most store-bought tomatoes are uniformly firm and flavourless, and unfortunately, the home-grown variety is available for such a short period that this recipe would be obsolete 11 months of the year if we based it on them.

As this chicken dish can also be served cold, it's excellent for picnics.

Serves 4.

1	3-pound (1.3-kg) chicken, cut into pieces, skin removed	1
2 teaspoons	salt	10 mL
½ teaspoon	freshly ground pepper	2 mL
3 tablespoons	oil	45 mL
1	large onion, coarsely chopped	1
2	cloves garlic, finely chopped	2
1	green OR red pepper, cut into strips lengthwise	1
1	28-ounce (800-mL) can tomatoes, drained and chopped OR 4 cups (1 L) fresh tomatoes, peeled, seeded, chopped	1
1 teaspoon	sugar	5 mL
3 tablespoons	ketchup	45 mL
1	bay leaf	1
1½ teaspoons	basil	7 mL
1 teaspoon	marjoram	5 mL

1. Sprinkle chicken pieces with salt and pepper.
2. In a frying pan or heavy skillet, heat oil over medium heat. Fry chicken, turning until all sides are golden. Remove pieces, drain on paper toweling and keep warm.
3. Drain all but about 1 tablespoon (15 mL) fat from pan. Over medium heat, sauté onion until transparent. Add garlic and green pepper and sauté an additional 30 seconds, stirring constantly.
4. Add tomatoes, sugar, ketchup, bay leaf, basil, and marjoram. Bring to boil.

5. Reduce heat and simmer, covered, 45 minutes.
6. Return chicken to pan; simmer, covered, an additional 30 minutes. Serve at once or let cool and chill to serve.

CHICKEN WITH YOGURT AND APRICOTS

Indian-inspired, this dish was created for The Best of Canada. *Serve to guests or family and you'll curry favour.*
Serves 4.

12	dried apricot halves	12
2 tablespoons	raisins	30 mL
³/₄ cup	Canadian port	175 mL
1	3-pound (1.3-kg) chicken	1
1 teaspoon	salt	5 mL
1 teaspoon	curry powder	5 mL
2 tablespoons	flour	30 mL
¹/₄ cup	unsalted butter	50 mL
1 tablespoon	finely chopped onion	15 mL
¹/₄ cup	dry white wine	50 mL
1 cup	yogurt	250 mL

1. Soak apricots and raisins in port for several hours.
2. Cut chicken into about 14 pieces. (Cut each leg and thigh into 3 pieces, and cut each halved breast into 4 pieces. Leave all bones in.)
3. Sprinkle chicken with salt and curry powder. Dredge with flour.
4. Melt butter in a sauté pan over medium heat. When foam subsides, sauté chicken pieces until golden on both sides. Remove chicken and set aside.
5. Drain excess fat from pan, and sauté onion until transparent.
6. Return chicken pieces to pan; increase heat, add white wine and deglaze pan by reducing liquid to half.
7. Reduce heat. Add yogurt, apricots, raisins, and port. Simmer, uncovered, 25 minutes. Serve at once.

SEVEN-DAY
TURKEY FEAST

Thanksgiving turkey is very much like a TV-mini series: it lasts a week, brings the family together, and becomes, for the most part, the overriding topic of conversation at work. But that tired and dried-out string of leftovers and picked-overs doesn't have to be.

We have created what might best be called a "game" plan, to help you happily put the Tom in your Tomorrow – and the next day, and the next – so you won't have to eat the same old dry, going drier, bits of turkey.

Here's a week of turkey meals that never repeats itself. Not once! The trick is to cut your turkey into the cuts required before you cook it. Using a 24-pound (10.8-kg) turkey, we created a whole week of different meals to feed a family of four.

The turkey feast starts with half the bird roasted, stuffed with walnuts and figs. The other half is reserved and cut into portions as required for the week's meals.

To prepare the turkey for the week-long turkey feast, cut the bird in half. First, make an incision down the breast. Then, using a boning knife, scrape breast flesh away from breast bone until you have two halves. Cut out and remove ribcage. Reserve bones for stock.

For roasted half turkey, remove leg bone leaving leg flesh attached to the body. This is a somewhat tricky manoeuvre, requiring the removal of all tendons. Proceed carefully.

For the other half of turkey: cut off the leg and wing, and skin the breast. Bone the leg as you did for the first half, and reserve wing for soup. Refrigerate for use during the week.

SEVEN-DAY MEAL PLAN:

DAY 1:
Roast Half-Turkey with Walnut-Fig Stuffing
Yam and Cranberry Casserole (page 161)
Zucchini Sautéed with Basil (page 162)

DAY 2:
Turkey Schnitzel Breaded with Walnuts OR
    Boneless Stuffed Turkey Leg
Celery Root Salad with Yogurt and Tarragon (page 171)

DAY 3:
Cordon Bleu Turkey Breast Stuffed with Spinach and
    Emmenthal Cheese
Lemon and Parsley Rice (page 185)
Yam and Chive Salad (page 168)

DAY 4:
Piccata of Turkey with Yogurt and Apricots OR
    Stir-Fried Turkey with Ginger and Bamboo Shoots
Onion, Orange, and Beet Salad (page 175)

DAY 5:
Paillard of Turkey
Golden Cauliflower (page 143)

DAY 6:
Medallions of Turkey in Oyster and Mushroom Sauce
Spinach and Pear Purée (page 153)

DAY 7:
Curried Turkey Soup

ROAST HALF TURKEY
WITH WALNUT-FIG STUFFING

DAY 1:

*Separate a 24-pound (10.8-kg) bird into halves (page 126).
Bone the leg.*

For your holiday dinner, this roasted half turkey will serve
12.

STUFFING:

1 cup	unsalted butter	250 mL
2 cups	chopped onion	500 mL
1 cup	diced celery	250 mL
1 cup	chopped walnuts	250 mL
2 tablespoons	chopped fresh parsley	30 mL
2 teaspoons	chopped fresh OR	10 mL
	½ teaspoon (2 mL) dried sage	
1 teaspoon	thyme	5 mL
1 teaspoon	basil	5 mL
8 cups	bread crumbs	2 L
2 teaspoons	salt	10 mL
1 teaspoon	freshly ground pepper	5 mL
2 teaspoons	powdered chicken stock	10 mL
¼ cup	Canadian port	50 mL
1 cup	chopped dried figs	250 mL
2	eggs	2
2 tablespoons	heavy (35%) cream	30 mL

½	24-pound (10.8-kg) turkey	½
¾ cup	oil	175 mL
1	onion	1
1	carrot	1

GRAVY:

1 or 2	chicken bouillon cubes	1 or 2
3 cups	boiling water	750 mL
	Pan drippings from roasted turkey	
1 tablespoon	cornstarch	15 mL

1. Melt butter in a large frying pan over medium heat. When foam subsides, sauté onion and celery until soft and golden.
2. Add walnuts, parsley, sage, thyme, and basil. Add bread crumbs, mix thoroughly, and cook 2 to 3 additional minutes. Add 1 teaspoon (5 mL) salt, pepper, and powdered chicken stock. Stir well. Remove from heat.
3. Sprinkle with port. Add figs and toss.
4. In a separate bowl, beat eggs and cream. Sprinkle over bread crumb mixture and mix thoroughly. Let cool.
5. Preheat oven to 375°F (190°C).
6. Sprinkle cavity of boned half-turkey with 1 teaspoon (5 mL) salt. Generously stuff leg and thigh cavity with cooled stuffing – about 4 cups (1 L) – until plump and firm. The turkey should look almost as though bone were back in. Cover and refrigerate remaining stuffing. Reserve for Boneless Stuffed Turkey Leg, Day 2, page 00.
7. Fold flap of breast flesh over stuffed cavity and pull firmly to underside of turkey. Secure by sewing with needle and thread. Tie wing down with string.
8. Pour ½ cup (125 mL) oil in roasting pan. Cut onion and carrot into 1-inch (2.5-cm) pieces and place in pan. (These vegetables add flavour to pan gravy, and they act as stilts for turkey, to prevent skin from sticking to hot pan.)
9. Rub turkey with remaining oil and sprinkle lightly with salt. Roast, uncovered, allowing 15 to 20 minutes per pound.
10. Baste with pan juices every 15 minutes, and turn bird over after about 1 ½ hours. If turkey starts to brown, cover with foil.
11. Remove from oven. Allow 5 to 10 minutes before slicing to permit juices to penetrate flesh.
12. To make gravy: Dissolve bouillon cubes in water. In a small saucepan, combine bouillon and pan drippings. Add cornstarch combined with enough water to make paste. Heat, stirring, until thickened. Serve hot.

TURKEY SCHNITZEL
BREADED WITH WALNUTS

DAY 2:

This dish requires cutting 2 slices from the widest part of the boned half of breast reserved for the week's dishes. Each slice should weigh about 3¹/₂ ounces (100 g).
    Serves 2.

2	slices of turkey breast, ¹/₂ inch (1.5 cm) thick	2
1	egg, lightly beaten	1
2 tablespoons	milk	30 mL
2 cups	bread crumbs	500 mL
¹/₄ cup	finely chopped walnuts	50 mL
	Flour seasoned with salt and pepper	
2 tablespoons	unsalted butter	30 mL

1. Using a mallet, flatten turkey slices between sheets of plastic wrap until paper thin. (The plastic wrap keeps the meat from sticking to the mallet, and it lets you see the progress you're making.)
2. In a bowl, beat egg and milk. In a separate bowl, thoroughly mix bread crumbs and walnuts. Dredge turkey slices with seasoned flour, dip in egg-milk mixture, and coat with walnut mixture.
3. In a sauté pan over medium heat, melt butter. When foam subsides, sauté schnitzel, about 4 minutes each side, or until browned. Serve at once.

BONELESS STUFFED TURKEY LEG

If you're not in the mood for turkey schnitzel, you may prefer to use the stuffing in your refrigerator and the boned turkey leg you put aside.
Serves 4.

1	boned turkey leg with thigh attached	1
	Salt	
3 to 4 cups	walnut-fig stuffing (from Day 1)	.75 to 1 L
⅓ cup	oil	75 mL
3	slices of raw carrot, 1 inch (2.5 cm) thick	3
3	slices of onion, 1 inch (2.5 cm) thick	3

1. Preheat oven to 375°F (190°C).
2. Sprinkle cavity of boned leg lightly with salt. Generously fill cavity with stuffing. Fold flap of leg and thigh flesh over stuffed cavity and pull firmly to underside of leg. Secure by sewing with needle and thread.
3. Pour oil in roasting pan and place slices of carrot and onion in pan. This gives flavour to pan juices and prevents skin of turkey from sticking to pan bottom.
4. Rub turkey lightly with 1 tablespoon (15 mL) oil and sprinkle lightly with salt. Roast, uncovered, about 1½ hours, or until golden brown. Baste every 15 minutes and turn over after about 40 minutes. If turkey browns too fast, cover with foil and continue to roast.
5. Remove from oven and let cool 10 minutes before slicing. Make gravy from pan juices (page 129).

CORDON BLEU TURKEY BREAST STUFFED WITH SPINACH AND EMMENTHAL CHEESE

DAY 3:

To prepare this dish, cut 2 pieces from the narrow end of the boned turkey breast.
Serves 2.

1/2	bunch spinach	1/2
2 tablespoons	unsalted butter	30 mL
1/4	clove garlic, finely chopped	1/4
	Salt and freshly ground pepper	
	Nutmeg to taste	
2	slices boned turkey breast, 3/4 inch (2 cm) thick	2
4	slices Canadian Emmenthal cheese	4
1	egg, lightly beaten	1
2 tablespoons	milk	30 mL
	Flour seasoned with salt and pepper	
1 cup	bread crumbs	250 mL

1. Preheat oven to 375°F (190°C).
2. Wash spinach and, without drying, place in small saucepan. Cook over medium heat, covered, without adding any water or butter, about 5 minutes, or until soft. Drain and set aside.
3. In a sauté pan over medium heat, melt 1 tablespoon (15 mL) butter. When foam subsides, sauté garlic until soft. Add spinach, salt, pepper, and nutmeg. Cook 2 to 3 minutes. Set aside.
4. Using mallet, flatten slices of turkey breast under plastic wrap until paper thin. At one end of each fillet, place slice of cheese. Cover with 2 tablespoons (30 mL) spinach mixture. Cover with second slice of cheese. Fold fillet and crimp edges.
5. In a separate bowl, mix egg and milk. Dredge turkey with seasoned flour, dip in egg-milk mixture, and coat all sides with bread crumbs.
6. In a sauté pan over medium heat, melt 1 tablespoon (15 mL) butter. When foam subsides, sauté turkey about 2 minutes per side.
7. Transfer to ovenproof casserole and bake 10 minutes, or until nicely puffed. Serve at once.

PICCATA OF TURKEY
WITH YOGURT AND APRICOTS

DAY 4:

Piccata *is an Italian term for a small, thinly sliced piece of meat, usually veal. Also known as scaloppine. For this dish, cut 6 very thin slices, about 1 ounce (30 g) each, from the breast fillet.*
    Serves 2.

6	**dried apricots**	6
6	**thin slices of turkey from breast, flattened with mallet**	6
	Flour seasoned with salt and pepper	
¼ cup	**unsalted butter**	50 mL
1 tablespoon	**finely chopped shallots OR onions**	15 mL
¼ cup	**Canadian port**	50 mL
3 tablespoons	**yogurt**	45 mL
3 tablespoons	**heavy (35%) cream**	45 mL
	Salt and freshly ground pepper	

1. Soften apricots in small amount of hot water.
2. Dredge slices of turkey with seasoned flour. In a sauté pan over medium heat, melt 2 tablespoons (30 mL) butter. When foam subsides, sauté turkey slices 2 to 3 minutes per side, or until lightly browned. Remove and set aside. Drain half the fat from the pan. Add shallots and sauté until golden.
3. Add port to deglaze pan. Add drained apricots. Reduce liquid to half.
4. Add yogurt, cream, salt, and pepper. Reduce liquid to half again, or until thick enough to coat a wooden spoon.
5. Add remaining butter to sauce and shake pan back and forth to incorporate butter; this will give gloss to sauce. Pour sauce over *piccata.* Serve 3 *piccata* per person.

STIR-FRIED TURKEY
WITH GINGER AND BAMBOO SHOOTS

If your piccata lunch wasn't enough to fill your appetite for turkey, we suggest a gloriously tasty, colourful, Chinese-style turkey dinner that uses only a pound (450 g) of meat and yet serves 4.

¼ cup	vegetable oil	50 mL
1 teaspoon	sesame oil	5 mL
1 pound	turkey breast cut into julienne strips	450 g
1 tablespoon	small sticks of fresh ginger root	15 mL
1 cup	sliced onions	250 mL
¼ pound	snow peas, trimmed	100 g
½ cup	bamboo shoots, drained	125 mL
2 cups	bean sprouts	500 mL
¼ cup	sweet rice wine	50 mL
2 tablespoons	soy sauce	30 mL
1 tablespoon	cornstarch	15 mL
2 tablespoons	water	30 mL

1. In a wok or large frying pan, heat vegetable oil and sesame oil over medium heat.
2. When oil is hot, add turkey strips, cooking about 4 minutes. Stir constantly. Drain and set aside.
3. Add ginger to wok. Gradually add onions, snow peas, bamboo shoots, and bean sprouts. Cook 3 to 4 minutes, but keep crisp. Return turkey to wok.
4. In a bowl, mix together wine and soy sauce. In a second bowl, mix cornstarch and water.
5. Add wine-soy mixture to saucepan and cook 2 additional minutes. Add cornstarch mixture, and cook until sauce thickens and clears. Season to taste.
6. Serve with Chinese noodles or rice.

PAILLARD OF TURKEY

DAY 5:

A paillard is an escalope of very thin breast that is broiled; ours is delicate and delicious, and goes perfectly with Golden Cauliflower (page 143).

Cut 2 very thin slices from the narrow end of the boned turkey breast.

Serves 2.

½ teaspoon	salt	2 mL
½ teaspoon	freshly ground pepper	2 mL
3 tablespoons	olive oil	45 mL
2 teaspoons	lemon juice	10 mL
2	slices boned turkey breast, ¾ inch (2 cm) thick, flattened slightly with mallet	2

1. Mix first 4 ingredients; marinate turkey slices in marinade for 2 hours.
2. Preheat broiler.
3. Remove turkey from marinade and place under preheated broiler; broil for about 3 minutes per side. Serve hot.

MEDALLIONS OF TURKEY
IN OYSTER AND MUSHROOM SAUCE

DAY 6:

The only thing longer than the name for this dish is the satisfaction you will have from eating it.

For this recipe, cut 2 thin pieces off the widest part of the ever-diminishing turkey breast.

Serves 2.

2	slices boned turkey breast, 3/4 inch (2 cm) thick, flattened slightly with a mallet	2
	Flour seasoned with salt and pepper	
2 tablespoons	unsalted butter	30 mL
1 tablespoon	finely chopped onion	15 mL
1 teaspoon	chopped parsley	5 mL
1 1/2 cups	sliced mushrooms	375 mL
2 tablespoons	brandy	30 mL
1/3 cup	heavy (35%) cream	75 mL
4	shucked oysters	4
	Chopped parsley, for garnish	

1. Dredge flattened pieces (medallions) of turkey with seasoned flour. In a sauté pan over medium heat, melt butter. When foam subsides, sauté turkey 3 minutes per side, turning only once. Cook until nicely browned. Remove and keep warm.
2. Drain half the butter from pan. Sauté onion until golden. Add parsley and sliced mushrooms and sauté 1 to 2 additional minutes.
3. Add brandy to deglaze pan. Reduce liquid to half. Add cream. Reduce liquid to half again, or until thick enough to coat wooden spoon.
4. Add shucked oysters and simmer 1 minute.
5. To serve, pour sauce onto plate; place hot medallions and oysters on top of sauce. Garnish with chopped parsley.

CURRIED TURKEY SOUP

DAY 7:

Whew! We made it: seven days of turkey and not one repeat. Here's a 7-days-later leftover soup that's just as tasty as anything that's gone before.

Yield: 8 to 10 cups (2 to 2.5 L).

	Turkey carcass and neck	
2 tablespoons	unsalted butter	30 mL
1 teaspoon	curry powder	5 mL
1	bay leaf	1
½ teaspoon	dried thyme	2 mL
2 tablespoons	chopped fresh parsley	30 mL
½ cup	chopped onion	125 mL
2 cups	diced celery	500 mL
2 cups	diced peeled potato	500 mL
1 cup	diced carrot	250 mL
1 cup	diced turnip	250 mL
	Any leftover turkey meat, cut into small pieces	
	Salt and freshly ground pepper	

1. Break turkey carcass into pieces and discard "parson's nose" at very end of bird. Place pieces and neck in a large soup pot. Cover with water and boil for 30 minutes.
2. Skim off fat. Remove bones and strain stock through cheesecloth. Pour stock into a soup pot and set aside.
3. Melt butter in a sauté pan over medium heat. When foam subsides, add curry powder, bay leaf, thyme, parsley, and all vegetables. Cook, covered, 8 minutes.
4. Add cooked vegetables to strained turkey stock. Also add any leftover turkey.
5. Bring stock to boil. Reduce heat and simmer, uncovered, 20 to 30 minutes, or until vegetables are just tender. Salt and pepper to taste. Serve hot.

VEGETABLES

FARMER'S ASPARAGUS, ST. LAWRENCE MARKET

Something delicious for one of the year's earliest vegetables.
Serves 4.

2 pounds	asparagus	1 kg
1 tablespoon	unsalted butter, melted	15 mL
1 cup	mayonnaise	250 mL
1/4 teaspoon	thyme	1 mL
1	tomato, peeled, seeded, diced	1
	Freshly ground pepper	
1/2	clove garlic, finely chopped	1/2
1/4 cup	grated Gruyère cheese	50 mL

1. Cut off and discard tough white bottoms of asparagus. Peel and wash stalks and tie in 4 bundles.
2. Cook asparagus in boiling, salted water to cover for about 8 minutes, or until tender, yet still firm.
3. Drain asparagus and pat dry with paper towels. Untie bundles.
4. Brush a shallow baking dish with melted butter. Place asparagus in baking dish with tips facing same direction.
5. Preheat broiler.
6. In a separate bowl, mix together mayonnaise, thyme, tomato, pepper, garlic, and cheese. Spread mixture evenly over asparagus. Place under preheated broiler on top oven rack; broil 1 to 2 minutes, or until sauce is browned. Serve at once.

GREEN BEANS IN
RED GARLIC SAUCE

Green or snap beans were formerly called string beans because they had a stringy filament that had to be removed. Not so the new hybrids.

Yellow beans may be used in this recipe, but we like the contrast of green beans in a red tomato sauce.

Serves 4 to 6.

1 pound	green beans, ends trimmed	450 g
1 tablespoon	unsalted butter	15 mL
2 tablespoons	finely chopped onion	30 mL
1	bay leaf	1
2	tomatoes, peeled, seeded, diced	2
1	clove garlic, finely chopped	1
2 tablespoons	dry white wine	30 mL
1 tablespoon	finely chopped parsley	15 mL
1 tablespoon	finely chopped fresh OR 1 teaspoon (5 mL) dried basil	15 mL
½ teaspoon	salt	2 mL
	Freshly ground pepper	
½ teaspoon	sugar	2 mL

1. Cook beans in a large pot of boiling, salted water for 7 minutes. Drain. Rinse under cold running water to set colour. Drain and set aside.
2. In a sauté pan over medium heat, melt butter. When foam subsides, sauté onion with bay leaf until onion is transparent.
3. Add tomatoes and garlic and sauté 1 additional minute.
4. Add wine, parsley, basil, salt, pepper, and sugar. Stir. Add blanched green beans. Reduce heat to low and simmer about 1 additional minute, or until beans are heated through. Serve at once.

BROCCOLI PURÉE

An original dish created for The Best of Canada, this might better be called Budget Broccoli. It takes little more than a bunch of broccoli and an onion; what you get is an elegant vegetable dish for dinner company.
Serves 4.

1 pound	broccoli	450 g
2 tablespoons	unsalted butter	30 mL
1	onion, chopped	1
1	clove garlic, crushed	1
1¼ cups	chicken stock	300 mL
1 teaspoon	salt	5 mL
	Freshly ground pepper	

1. Wash and trim broccoli; cut into flowerets; peel and cut stem into pieces.
2. In a large saucepan over medium heat, melt 1 tablespoon (15 mL) butter. When foam subsides, sauté onion until transparent. Add garlic, broccoli, chicken stock, salt, and pepper. Bring to boil.
3. Reduce heat and simmer, covered, 15 to 20 minutes, or until broccoli is tender.
4. Purée mixture in food processor or blender. Add 1 tablespoon (15 mL) butter; mix in well. Salt and pepper to taste. Serve hot.

BEST-EVER BROCCOLI

Tony makes the broccoli; I make the claim. The recipe calls for very finely chopped onion. I noticed Tony in action, drawing his knife across the onion with extreme care; he did not make bold chopping cuts. When asked why, the chef said that a coarse chopping action actually ruptures membranes, causing a chemical change that sours the onion.
Serves 4.

1 tablespoon	oil	15 mL
1/2	medium-sized onion, very finely chopped	1/2
1 1/4 cups	diced canned tomatoes	300 mL
1/4 teaspoon	oregano	1 mL
	Freshly ground pepper	
1/2 teaspoon	sugar	2 mL
1 teaspoon	celery salt	5 mL
1 pound	broccoli, cut into flowerets, stem sliced into pieces	450 g
	Salt and pepper to taste	
1/4 cup	grated old Canadian Cheddar cheese	50 mL

1. In a sauté pan, heat oil over medium heat. Sauté onion until soft and transparent.
2. Add tomatoes, oregano, pepper, sugar, celery salt, and broccoli. Stir.
3. Reduce heat and simmer, uncovered, 8 to 12 minutes; keep broccoli crisp. Salt and pepper to taste. Preheat broiler.
4. Transfer broccoli to ovenproof casserole. Sprinkle with grated Cheddar and place under preheated broiler until golden.

GOLDEN CAULIFLOWER

Serves 4.

1	medium-sized cauliflower	1
2	eggs	2
	Salt to taste	
1/2 cup	oil	125 mL

1. Wash cauliflower. Trim leaves, discard stem, and separate into flowerets. Blanch in a large pot of boiling salted water 4 to 5 minutes, or until tender-crisp. Drain.
2. Cut flowerets in half lengthwise and dry on paper towels.
3. In a bowl, beat eggs with salt.
4. In a frying pan, heat oil over medium heat. Dip flowerets into beaten eggs and fry, turning occasionally, until golden. Serve hot.

BRADFORD BRUSSELS SPROUTS

A new dish created especially for The Best of Canada, *named after the area north of Toronto where the sprouts grow green as crabgrass – and just about as fast.*
Serves 4 to 6.

1 pound	Brussels sprouts	450 g
3 tablespoons	unsalted butter	45 mL
1	clove garlic, finely chopped	1
¼ teaspoon	thyme	1 mL
1 teaspoon	soy sauce	5 mL

1. Cut sprouts diagonally, making 4 or 5 slices out of each small sprout.
2. Blanch sprouts in boiling, salted water to cover for about 3 minutes, or until tender-crisp.
3. Drain and rinse under cold running water to stop cooking and to set colour. Drain and set aside.
4. Melt butter in a large frying pan over medium heat. When foam subsides, lightly sauté garlic. Add blanched sprouts, thyme, and soy sauce, and sauté about 10 minutes. Keep sprouts crisp. Serve hot.

CABBAGE SAUTÉED WITH CUMIN

Serves 4.

3 tablespoons	oil	45 mL
1	large onion, thinly sliced	1
1	medium-sized cabbage, cored, shredded	1
½ teaspoon	thyme	2 mL
½ teaspoon	cumin seed, crushed	2 mL
1	clove garlic, finely chopped	1
1½ teaspoons	salt	7 mL
	Freshly ground pepper	

1. In a sauté pan, heat oil over medium heat. Sauté onion until transparent.
2. Add cabbage, thyme, and cumin seed. Increase heat to medium-high and sauté about 10 minutes. Stir frequently to prevent burning.
3. Add garlic and sauté 1 additional minute. Add salt and pepper to taste. Serve at once.

STEWED RED CABBAGE WITH APPLE AND WINE

Serves 6.

5	slices bacon, cut into 1-inch (2.5-cm) pieces	5
1	large onion, sliced	1
1	small apple, quartered, cored, sliced	1
4 cups	finely shredded red cabbage (about ½ medium-sized cabbage)	1 L
½ cup	wine vinegar	125 mL
1 cup	water	250 mL
½ cup	dry red wine	125 mL
1	bay leaf	1
1	clove	1
1½ teaspoons	salt	7 mL
¼ teaspoon	freshly ground pepper	1 mL
2 tablespoons	sugar	30 mL

1. In a saucepan over medium heat, fry bacon until transparent. Add onion and apple and sauté an additional 3 to 4 minutes, or until onion is transparent.
2. Add remaining ingredients. Mix thoroughly. Bring to boil, reduce heat and simmer, covered, for 1 hour. Serve hot.

KOHLRABI WITH BÉCHAMEL SAUCE

Kohlrabi is an offshoot of the cabbage clan that is gaining popularity across Canada. Cooks who are looking for new tastes have been experimenting with these plants.

You may not find kohlrabi in large supermarkets, but check ethnic food stores in early summer.

Serves 4.

2	kohlrabi	2
1 cup	béchamel sauce (page 215)	250 mL
¼ cup	chicken stock	50 mL
⅓ cup	grated old Canadian Cheddar cheese	75 mL
1 tablespoon	chopped fresh chives	15 mL

1. Preheat oven to 400°F (200°C). Trim tops and bottoms of kohlrabi. Peel the bulb and cut into thick julienne sticks.
2. Blanch kohlrabi in boiling, salted water to cover for 3 minutes. Drain. Transfer to baking dish.
3. In a saucepan over medium heat, slowly warm béchamel sauce. Add chicken stock, 3 tablespoons (45 mL) grated Cheddar cheese, and chives. Mix and heat thoroughly.
4. Pour hot sauce over kohlrabi. Bake 25 minutes. Sprinkle with remaining cheese. Place under preheated broiler until golden. Serve at once.

RAPTUROUS RAPINI

Rapini is a member of the cabbage family well-loved by Canada's Italian population. They also call it broccolirab, and it's known by other names, such as rape and cole.

The leaves of the rapini have a very strong, identifiable, somewhat bitter taste. The stalks, about 6 inches long, are green to bluish in colour. Fresh rapini has small green flowers; yellow flowers mean the plant is aged.

An ideal accompaniment for strong meats, especially pork and sausage dishes.

Serves 4.

146

1 pound	rapini	450 g
2 tablespoons	unsalted butter	30 mL
2	slices bacon, cut into thin strips	2
1/2	clove garlic, crushed	1/2
2 tablespoons	tarragon vinegar OR 1/2 teaspoon (2 mL) dried tarragon mixed with 2 tablespoons (30 mL) vinegar	30 mL
	Salt and freshly ground pepper	

1. Cut and discard tough outer leaves and tough stems of rapini. Separate leaves from stalk; discard stalk and wash leaves well. Cook leaves in boiling, salted water to cover, covered, about 15 minutes. Drain and keep warm.
2. In a frying pan over medium heat, melt butter. When foam subsides, sauté bacon until crisp. Add garlic and tarragon vinegar. Bring to boil and reduce liquid to half.
3. Pour bacon-garlic sauce over rapini. Salt and pepper to taste. Serve hot.

PAN-FRIED CUCUMBER WITH DILL

A glorious garnish for almost all fish dishes.
Serves 2.

1 cup	julienne sticks of cucumber (method below)	250 mL
2 cups	water	500 mL
1 1/2 teaspoons	salt	7 mL
3	sprigs fresh OR 1 teaspoon (5 mL) dried dill	3
2 tablespoons	unsalted butter	30 mL
2 teaspoons	finely chopped dill	10 mL
	Salt to taste	

1. Peel cucumber, trim ends, and cut in half lengthwise. Scoop out seeds using spoon. Cut halves into pieces about 2 inches (5 cm) long. Cut pieces lengthwise into small sticks.

2. In a pot, bring water to a boil. Add salt and dill sprigs. Blanch cucumber for 2 minutes. Drain and rinse under cold running water to set colour. Drain and set aside.
3. Melt butter in a saucepan over medium heat. When foam subsides, sauté blanched cucumber about 2 minutes. Sprinkle with dill. Salt to taste. Serve at once.

JULIA'S POTATO WAFFLES

These are grand and garlicky potatoes that can be baked in 35 minutes. Tony's mother, Julia, was making them back in the days when the family lived in France – when the only thing Tony was making was mud pies.

The potato waffles are perfect with a roast, broiled lamb, our 1929 Hamburger (page 87), or our Mighty Midweek Meat Loaf (page 90).

Serves 4.

4	large P.E.I. potatoes, scrubbed, *not* peeled	4
1 tablespoon	olive oil	15 mL
1	clove garlic, crushed	1
1 teaspoon	coarse salt	5 mL
1 teaspoon	coarsely ground pepper	5 mL

1. Preheat oven to 400°F (200°C).
2. Cut potatoes in half lengthwise. Using a knife, make 3 diagonal cuts across potato face about ½ inch (1.5 cm) in depth. Then make 3 more diagonal cuts that run at right angles to first cuts. Potato face will look a bit like a waffle – hence the name for this dish.
3. Coat bottom of roasting pan with oil. Add garlic, salt, and pepper.
4. Set potatoes in pan face down; rub them in oil-garlic mixture.
5. Bake 35 minutes or until golden. (Even if you get lost in the preparation of another dish, these potatoes do not burn even after an hour because of the oil.) Serve hot.

POTATO AND TURNIP CASSEROLE

Serves 4.

2	large potatoes, peeled, quartered, and thinly sliced	2
2	large turnips, tops and bottoms discarded, peeled, quartered, and thinly sliced	2
1	large onion, peeled, cut in half lengthwise, halves sliced thin	1
1 tablespoon	finely chopped parsley	15 mL
2 tablespoons	flour	30 mL
1 teaspoon	salt	5 mL
1/4 teaspoon	freshly ground pepper	1 mL
1/8 teaspoon	nutmeg	0.5 mL
1/4 teaspoon	thyme	1 mL
3/4 cup	grated Emmenthal cheese	175 mL
2 cups	milk	500 mL
1	egg, lightly beaten	1
2 tablespoons	unsalted butter	30 mL
1	bay leaf	1

1. Preheat oven to 400°F (200°C).
2. In a large bowl, combine potatoes, turnips, onion, parsley, flour, salt, pepper, nutmeg, thyme, and 1/2 cup (125 mL) grated cheese. Toss well.
3. In a separate bowl, mix milk and egg. Pour over potato-turnip mixture. Mix well.
4. Transfer mixture to well-greased ovenproof casserole. Dot with butter and crown with bay leaf. Bake, uncovered, 1 1/2 hours. Remove bayleaf.
5. Sprinkle with 1/4 cup (50 mL) grated cheese. Brown top under preheated broiler for about 30 seconds and serve at once.

P.E.I. POTATO PIE

This pie, an original creation for the book, can be served hot or cold and goes well with salads. Layers of potato and leek are mounded in pyramid fashion underneath a golden pie crust. Before cutting, the pie resembles a plentifully packed apple pie.
  Serves 6 to 8.

	Dough for 9-inch (1-L) double-crust pie (page 207)	

FILLING:

5	medium-sized potatoes, peeled, sliced very thin	5
½ teaspoon	salt	2 mL
½ teaspoon	freshly ground pepper	2 mL
1 tablespoon	finely chopped parsley	15 mL
½ teaspoon	thyme	2 mL
1	large leek, white and light green portion only, finely chopped	1
1	medium-sized onion, very finely chopped	1
2 tablespoons	unsalted butter, melted	30 mL
½ pound	Canadian Emmenthal cheese, thinly sliced	225 g
4	slices ham	4
1	egg yolk mixed with 1 tablespoon (15 mL) milk	1

1. Preheat oven to 400°F (200°C).
2. Line a 9-inch (1-L) pie pan with half the pastry dough. Pierce dough with fork and bake 10 minutes. Lower heat to 350°F (180°C) and bake an additional 5 minutes. Remove and cool.
3. Meanwhile, combine potatoes, salt, pepper, parsley, and thyme. Toss well. Cover cooled pie shell with a layer of seasoned potato slices – not all will be used. Overlap slices to completely cover crust; no dough should be visible.
4. In a separate bowl, mix leek and onion. Sprinkle half the mixture over potatoes. Sprinkle with 1 tablespoon (15 mL) melted butter.

5. Using half the cheese slices, make a layer of cheese. Buttress slices edge to edge. Cover with layer of ham, using all 4 slices.
6. Cover ham with remaining cheese.
7. Sprinkle with 1 tablespoon (15 mL) melted butter. Add a second layer of potatoes and another layer of leek-onion. Crown with a final layer of potatoes. Shape pie like a cone, placing more ingredients toward centre than at edge. You now have an 8-layered cone rising dramatically at the middle.
8. Preheat oven to 400°F (200°C).
9. Cover pie with top crust and crimp edges. Pierce crust with fork for steam vents. Brush with eggwash. Bake 1½ hours, or until crust is golden; if shell browns too quickly, cover with foil and complete baking.
10. Using cake tester or needle, check potatoes. When soft and cooked through, remove pie from oven. Serve hot or cold.

MANITOBA MASHED POTATOES

Serves 6.

5	large potatoes	5
2 tablespoons	unsalted butter	30 mL
½ cup	heavy (35%) cream	125 mL
¾ cup	milk	175 mL
½ teaspoon	salt	2 mL
	Pinch of nutmeg	

1. To prepare potatoes, peel and cut into large pieces. Cook, covered, in boiling, salted water to cover for 20 minutes, or until potatoes are soft. Drain well.
2. In a bowl, using an electric mixer, mash potatoes well. Add butter, cream, milk, salt, and nutmeg. Continue mixing until potatoes are light and smooth.
3. Transfer to saucepan and heat, stirring constantly. Serve when hot.

DESIGNER LABEL STUFFED SPUDS

A dish that elevates the humble potato to fashion-status food. You may even wish to make your whole dinner fancy, as these spuds come to the table dressed formally — in their jackets.
Serves 8.

4	large P.E.I. potatoes, scrubbed	4
1 tablespoon	unsalted butter	15 mL
2 tablespoons	finely chopped onion	30 mL
2 tablespoons	finely chopped parsley	30 mL
½ cup	sour cream	125 mL
½ cup	grated Cheddar cheese	125 mL
	Pinch of nutmeg	
1 teaspoon	salt	5 mL
	Freshly ground pepper	

1. Preheat oven to 375°F (190°C). Bake potatoes, unwrapped, about 1 hour, or until tender. Remove and set aside. Lower oven setting to 350°F (180°C).
2. Melt butter in a sauté pan over medium heat. When foam subsides, sauté onion until transparent. Stir in parsley, heat through, and set aside.
3. Cut baked potatoes in half lengthwise. Scoop out pulp and place in large mixing bowl. Be careful not to tear jackets.
4. To pulp, add sour cream, ¼ cup (50 mL) grated Cheddar, nutmeg, salt, and pepper. Mix thoroughly. Stuff mixture into potato skins. Bake, uncovered, at 350°F (180°C) about 20 minutes, or until hot.
5. Sprinkle with remaining grated cheese; place under pre-heated broiler until golden. Serve at once.

POTATO 'N' TOMATO

We prefer new potatoes for this dish, but any old spud'll do.
Serves 4 to 6.

1 tablespoon	unsalted butter	15 mL
1	large onion, finely chopped	1
1	large tomato, peeled, seeded, diced	1
6	medium-sized potatoes, peeled, quartered, cut into thin slices	6
1¾ cups	chicken stock	425 mL
1	bay leaf	1
1 teaspoon	paprika	5 mL
2 teaspoons	finely chopped parsley	10 mL
1 teaspoon	salt	5 mL
½ teaspoon	freshly ground pepper	2 mL

1. Melt butter in a saucepan over medium heat. When foam subsides, sauté onion until transparent.
2. Add tomato and sauté 1 additional minute. Add remaining ingredients and bring to boil. Reduce heat and simmer, uncovered, 45 minutes or until potatoes are tender. Serve hot.

SPINACH AND PEAR PURÉE

This is a tasty garnish that goes with everything – fish, veal, chicken.
Serves 2.

2	bunches spinach OR half a 10-ounce (285-g) bag	2
½	pear, peeled, sliced	½
1 tablespoon	lemon juice	15 mL
1 tablespoon	light or heavy cream	15 mL
1 tablespoon	unsalted butter	15 mL
	Salt and freshly ground pepper	

1. Wash spinach; do not shake off excess water.
2. In a saucepan over medium heat, cook spinach with pear until spinach is soft. Do not add additional water. Drain.
3. Transfer spinach and pear to a blender or a food processor fitted with steel blade. Purée.
4. Add remaining ingredients. Purée until smooth. Chill to serve.

BRAISED LEEK WITH VERMOUTH

A delicious and quick-to-prepare recipe. Perfect with eggs or a great appetizer by itself.
  Serves 2.

8	leeks, white and light green portion only, well washed	8
1 tablespoon	unsalted butter	15 mL
¼ cup	sweet Canadian vermouth	50 mL
1 tablespoon	cider vinegar	15 mL
1 tablespoon	soy sauce	15 mL
	Salt	
	Freshly ground white pepper	

1. Cut leeks into pieces 2 inches (5 cm) long. Cook in boiling, salted water to cover 8 to 10 minutes or until tender-crisp. Keep leeks crunchy. Drain. Set aside.
2. Melt butter in a saucepan over medium heat. When foam subsides, sauté leeks 1 minute. Add vermouth, vinegar, and soy sauce. Reduce heat and simmer until nearly all liquid has evaporated.
3. Season to taste with salt and white pepper. Serve at once.

ONIONS IN SOUR CREAM SAUCE

A perfect vegetable for pork and beef dishes.
  Serves 3 to 4.

6	onions, peeled, cut in half lengthwise	6
2 tablespoons	unsalted butter	30 mL
⅓ cup	sour cream	75 mL
¼ cup	dry white wine	50 mL
¼ teaspoon	cumin	1 mL
¼ teaspoon	salt	1 mL
	Paprika to taste	

1. Blanch onions in boiling, salted water to cover for about 2 minutes. Drain and pat onions dry.
2. In same saucepan over medium heat, melt butter. When foam subsides, sauté onion halves until fully golden. Add sour cream, wine, cumin, and salt. Stir.
3. Add paprika and simmer for about 15 minutes or until onions are tender.

GINGERED CARROTS

This dish could be called Carrots Supreme; it is supremely simple to make, supremely sweet to taste. The maple syrup is a truly Canadian touch that complements ginger's identifiable zing.
Serves 3 to 4.

2 tablespoons	unsalted butter	30 mL
½	onion, finely chopped	½
1 pound	carrots, peeled, sliced	450 g
1 tablespoon	crystallized ginger, finely chopped (page 222) OR 2 teaspoons (10 mL) grated fresh ginger root	15 mL
¼ cup	maple syrup	50 mL
½ cup	water	125 mL
½ teaspoon	salt	2 mL
1 teaspoon	finely chopped parsley	5 mL

1. Melt butter in a sauté pan over medium heat. When foam subsides, sauté onion until transparent. Add carrots, ginger, maple syrup, water, and salt.
2. Cook about 30 minutes, stirring occasionally, until carrots are just tender. Sprinkle with parsley and serve at once.

CARDOON AT MIDNOON

Sounds like a stilted operetta or spaghetti western, doesn't it? Actually, cardoon is a little-known, white-green, thistle-like plant that prefers warmer climes. It will be found in some of our ethnic – particularly Italian – markets.

Cardoon might indeed go well at noon, for the edible stalks and leafy midribs look like celery, which is commonly eaten at midday. Nevertheless, the vegetable tastes more like an artichoke, to which it is a cookable cousin.

Cardoon grown in North America takes longer to cook and soften than the variety grown in Europe. Since it discolours quickly upon being cut, we suggest pieces be kept in a pot of acidulated water (about 2 tablespoons [30 mL] lemon juice OR vinegar to each 4 cups [1 L] water) until used.

Tony likes to boil cardoon with a bit of flour; this technique helps to keep the pieces light in colour.

If you can't find cardoon in your local market, substitute celery. Blanch celery pieces in boiling water for 15 minutes or until tender; drain and use as cardoon in the rest of this recipe.

Serves 4 to 6.

1 pound	edible stalks and leafy ribs of cardoon	450 g
8 cups	water	2 L
1 tablespoon	salt	15 mL
2 tablespoons	flour	30 mL
	Juice of 1 lemon	
¼ cup	unsalted butter	50 mL
4	slices bacon, cut into pieces	4
2	cloves garlic, finely chopped	2
2 tablespoons	finely chopped parsley	30 mL
½ teaspoon	oregano	2 mL
¼ cup	dry white wine	50 mL
½ cup	heavy (35%) cream	125 mL
2 tablespoons	soy sauce	30 mL
	Pepper	

1. Wash and scrub cardoon stalks and ribs; discard any stringy bits. Cut cardoon into pieces 2 inches (5 cm) long.

2. In a large pot, bring water to a boil. Add salt, flour, and lemon juice; add cardoon. Bring to boil again. Reduce heat and simmer, covered, up to 1½ hours or until tender. Drain. Set aside.
3. In a sauté pan over medium heat, melt butter. When foam subsides, sauté bacon until crisp. Add cooked cardoon (OR blanched celery) and sauté an additional 30 seconds.
4. Add garlic, parsley, and oregano and sauté 1 additional minute, stirring constantly.
5. Add wine and cook until all liquid evaporates. Add cream, soy sauce, and pepper. Reduce liquid to half. Pepper to taste. Serve at once.

CALGARY CORN FRITTERS

Yield: 12 fritters.

2	eggs, beaten	2
5 tablespoons	flour	75 mL
1 teaspoon	baking powder	5 mL
1 tablespoon	finely chopped onion	15 mL
	Freshly ground pepper	
½ teaspoon	salt	2 mL
3 tablespoons	peeled, shredded sweet potato	45 mL
1½ cups	fresh corn kernels OR drained, canned kernel corn	375 mL
2 tablespoons	corn oil	30 mL

1. In a bowl, beat eggs lightly; add flour and baking powder. Mix well.
2. Add onion, pepper, salt, sweet potato, and corn. Mix thoroughly. Let mixture rest for 30 minutes.
3. In a frying pan, heat 1 tablespoon oil over medium-high heat. When hot, spoon batter into pan, making small fritters about 3 inches (8 cm) in diameter. Fritters must not touch one another. Fry until golden brown on bottom, about 4 to 5 minutes. Flip and fry other side until golden.
4. Repeat procedure, using all batter and replenishing oil as required.
5. Keep fritters wrapped in paper towels in a warm oven until all are cooked. Serve hot.

TOMATOES STUFFED
WITH CHEESE MOUSSE

Great for the family yet elegant for company. Margarith, Tony's wife, created this dish one Sunday afternoon using ingredients that were left over from our recipe experimentation.
Serves 4.

4	medium-sized tomatoes	4
1	large egg, separated	1
½ cup	grated Canadian Emmenthal cheese	125 mL
1 tablespoon	heavy (35%) cream	15 mL
1 tablespoon	finely chopped chives	15 mL
	Freshly grated nutmeg to taste	
	Salt and freshly ground pepper	

1. Cut tops off tomatoes and set aside. Scoop out pulp and save for another use. Invert tomatoes 10 minutes to drain.
2. Preheat oven to 400°F (200°C).
3. In a bowl, beat egg yolk with grated cheese. Add heavy cream, chives, and nutmeg; mix well. Add salt and pepper to taste.
4. In a separate bowl, beat egg white until stiff; fold gently into cheese mixture.
5. Lightly sprinkle insides of tomatoes with salt. Stuff each tomato with cheese mixture and recap with tops.
6. Transfer tomatoes to a baking dish. Bake 20 to 25 minutes.

SCALLOPED TURNIPS

This recipe calls for 5 cups (1.2 L) thinly sliced turnips. To help estimate your needs, 1 pound (450 g) whole turnips yields about 3¹/₂ cups (875 mL) raw, sliced vegetable.
Serves 4 to 6.

5 cups	thinly sliced turnips (method below)	1.2 L
3 tablespoons	flour	45 mL
1 tablespoon	chopped parsley	15 mL
1	medium-sized onion, thinly sliced	1
	Freshly ground pepper	
	Freshly grated nutmeg	
1 teaspoon	salt	5 mL
¹/₄ cup	grated Parmesan cheese	50 mL
1	egg, beaten	1
1 cup	milk	250 mL
³/₄ cup	heavy (35%) cream	175 mL
2 tablespoons	unsalted butter	30 mL

1. Cut off and discard turnip tops; peel and quarter turnips; thinly slice.
2. Preheat oven to 400°F (200°C).
3. In a bowl, combine turnip slices, flour, parsley, onion, pepper, nutmeg, salt, and 2 tablespoons (30 mL) Parmesan cheese. Mix well.
4. Transfer mixture to well-greased 1¹/₂-quart (1.5-L) oven-proof casserole.
5. In a separate bowl, mix together egg, milk, and cream; pour over turnip mixture. Dot top with butter. Bake, uncovered, 50 minutes, or until done.
6. Sprinkle with remaining Parmesan cheese and place under preheated broiler until golden.

FENNEL WITH LEMON AND CHEESE

Finocchio, as Italians call fresh fennel, has a delicious, distinctive flavour, something akin to licorice or anise. The bulbous vegetable looks like a swollen celery. It can be enjoyed raw or cooked.

Finocchio is growing in popularity in Canada and can now be found in winter months in some major supermarkets. Serves 4.

2	medium-sized finocchio (fennel) bulbs	2
4 cups	water	1 L
2 teaspoons	salt	10 mL
	Juice of 1 lemon	
2 tablespoons	unsalted butter	30 mL
2 tablespoons	grated Canadian Emmenthal cheese	30 mL

1. Cut and discard feathery tops of fennel; cut off hard bottom, and discard tough outer stalks. Separate inner bulb stalks and cut in half or quarters lengthwise.
2. In a saucepan, bring water, salt and juice of ½ lemon to a boil. Add fennel and cook, uncovered, about 5 minutes, keeping some crunch in the fennel. Drain and transfer fennel to ovenproof dish and set aside. Preheat broiler.
3. Melt butter in a sauté pan over medium heat. When hot, add juice of ½ lemon. Mix well. Pour hot sauce over fennel. Sprinkle with grated cheese and place under preheated broiler until golden in colour. Serve at once.

YAM AND APPLE OMELETTE

Here's an omelette made without eggs. We got our best results using an omelette pan because the sloping sides eased sliding the "omelette" out of the pan – a necessary step.

A great brunch item, or a novel dish with poultry entrées. Serves 2.

1½ cups	peeled, shredded yam	375 mL
1	medium-sized apple, peeled, cored, coarsely chopped	1

⅓ cup	diced ham	75 mL
2 tablespoons	flour	30 mL
½ teaspoon	salt	2 mL
	Freshly ground pepper	
3 tablespoons	unsalted butter	45 mL

1. In a bowl, mix first 6 ingredients well.
2. In an omelette pan or non-stick frying pan, melt half the butter over medium heat. When foam subsides, add yam-apple mixture. Scramble mixture with spatula; as it heats through, flatten it down.
3. Cook about 10 minutes or until golden crust forms on bottom. Slide omelette onto a plate.
4. Add remaining butter to pan, flip omelette (between two plates) and return to pan, cooking second side about 5 minutes or until golden brown. Slide out of pan onto plate and serve.

YAM AND CRANBERRY CASSEROLE

Serves 5.

4 cups	thinly sliced, peeled yam halves	1 L
1 cup	whole raw cranberries	250 mL
¾ cup	finely sliced onion	175 mL
1½ cups	heavy (35%) cream	375 mL
1	egg, lightly beaten	1
½ teaspoon	salt	2 mL
¼ teaspoon	freshly ground pepper	1 mL
	Nutmeg to taste	
¼ cup	grated Parmesan cheese	50 mL

1. Preheat oven to 375°F (190°C).
2. In an ovenproof casserole, combine yam, cranberries, and onion.
3. In a separate bowl, mix cream, egg, salt, pepper, and nutmeg. Pour over yam-cranberry mixture and mix thoroughly.
4. Bake, uncovered, 20 minutes. Cover and bake additional 25 to 30 minutes. Remove cover. Sprinkle with Parmesan cheese, and return to oven for 5 minutes, or until cheese melts.

ZUCCHINI SAUTÉED WITH BASIL

Serves 4.

2 tablespoons	unsalted butter	30 mL
1	medium-sized onion, diced	1
1	clove garlic, crushed	1
3	medium-sized zucchini, thinly sliced	3
1	medium-sized tomato, coarsely chopped	1
1 teaspoon	chopped fresh OR dried basil	5 mL
1 teaspoon	chopped fresh OR dried thyme	5 mL
	Salt and freshly ground pepper	

1. Melt butter in a sauté pan over medium heat. When foam subsides, sauté onion with garlic until golden. Add zucchini and sauté 2 additional minutes.
2. Add tomato and cook 2 additional minutes. Stir to prevent burning. Sprinkle with basil, thyme, salt, and pepper. Stir. Serve hot.

ZUCCHINI FRITTERS

Serves 4.

2	eggs	2
1 tablespoon	milk	15 mL
3 tablespoons	sesame seeds	45 mL
3 tablespoons	bread crumbs	45 mL
1 tablespoon	finely chopped parsley	15 mL
1 tablespoon	grated onion	15 mL
½ teaspoon	oregano	2 mL
2	small zucchini, thinly sliced	2
3 tablespoons	flour	45 mL
	Oil for deep-frying	
	Salt and freshly ground pepper	

1. In a bowl, mix eggs and milk. In a separate bowl, combine sesame seeds, bread crumbs, parsley, onion, and oregano.
2. Dredge zucchini slices with flour. Dip slices into egg-milk batter, then dredge with sesame-seed mixture.
3. Heat oil to 365°F (185°C). Deep-fry zucchini until crisp and golden. Drain on paper towelling. Season with salt and pepper and serve immediately.

ZUCCHINI À LA KING CITY

When we were three-quarters through writing this book, Tony realized that he'd forgotten to name even one dish after the town he lives in, on the fringe of Toronto.

And so we present this vegetable creation, made with zucchini from Tony's green (and weedy) garden in King City.
Serves 4.

1 pound	zucchini	450 g
¼ cup	olive oil	50 mL
½ cup	finely chopped onion	125 mL
1	clove garlic, finely chopped	1
1 tablespoon	finely chopped fresh basil OR 1 teaspoon (5 mL) dried	15 mL
½ cup	dry white wine	125 mL
	Salt	
¼ teaspoon	freshly ground pepper	1 mL
1 tablespoon	finely chopped parsley	15 mL

1. Cut zucchini into quarters lengthwise; cut each quarter into slices ¼ inch (0.75 cm) thick.
2. In a sauté pan, heat oil over medium heat. Sauté onion until transparent. Add zucchini and garlic and sauté an additional 5 minutes.
3. Add basil, white wine, salt, and pepper. Simmer, covered, about 8 minutes.
4. Garnish with parsley for colour and taste.

STUFFED EGGPLANT
DANFORTH-STYLE

This dish is so named because it is basically a Greek-style dish, and we can't think of any place in Canada more Greek than Toronto's Danforth Avenue.

An original dish for The Best of Canada.

Serves 2.

1	**medium-sized eggplant**	1
2 teaspoons	**unsalted butter**	10 mL
2 tablespoons	**finely chopped onion**	30 mL
1	**clove garlic, finely chopped**	1
½	**tomato, peeled, seeded, diced**	½
¼	**red pepper, very finely diced**	¼
2 tablespoons	**fresh bread crumbs**	30 mL
½ teaspoon	**oregano**	2 mL
¼ cup	**grated Parmesan cheese**	50 mL
1 tablespoon	**finely chopped parsley**	15 mL
1 teaspoon	**powdered chicken stock**	5 mL
½ teaspoon	**salt**	2 mL
	Freshly ground pepper	
1	**egg, separated**	1

1. Preheat oven to 350°F (180°C).
2. Cut eggplant in half lengthwise and place cut-side up in well-greased baking dish. Bake 30 minutes or until pulp is tender. Remove from oven. Increase heat to 425°F (220°C).
3. Using a spoon, remove pulp to within ¼ inch (0.75 cm) of skin. Do not cut or blemish skins. Reserve skins. Chop pulp very finely and set aside to cool.
4. Melt butter in a sauté pan over medium heat. When foam subsides, sauté onion until transparent. Add garlic, tomato, and red pepper, and sauté an additional 30 seconds. Remove from heat.
5. Add bread crumbs, oregano, Parmesan cheese, parsley, powdered chicken stock, salt, and pepper. Mix well. Transfer to mixing bowl.
6. Add chopped eggplant pulp to onion-tomato mixture and mix thoroughly. Let cool.
7. When cool, blend in egg yolk. To this point, dish can be prepared in advance.
8. In a separate bowl, beat egg white until stiff. Fold gently into eggplant mixture. Spoon mixture into eggplant skins. Bake 15 minutes. Serve hot.

SALADS

ABC SALAD
(APPLE-BEET-CARROT SALAD)

A very simple, very satisfying salad.
    Serves 6.

3	large beets	3
4	medium-sized carrots	4
1	large apple, preferably McIntosh, peeled, cored, quartered, sliced	1
1/3 cup	olive oil	75 mL
3 tablespoons	cider vinegar	45 mL
3 tablespoons	finely diced onion	45 mL
1 teaspoon	salt	5 mL
	Freshly ground pepper	

1. Trim beet tops. Drop beets in boiling, salted water to cover and cook, uncovered, until tender, about 30 to 60 minutes. Drain and rinse under cold running water to set colour. Drain; rub off skin. When beets are cool, quarter and cut into slices. Set aside.
2. Peel carrots and cut into thin slices. Drop carrot slices into boiling salted water to cover and cook, uncovered, 10 minutes, or until tender. Drain and rinse under cold running water. Drain. Cool.
3. In a bowl, combine and toss beet, carrot, and apple slices.
4. In a separate bowl, mix together olive oil, vinegar, onion, salt, and pepper to make vinaigrette. Pour over apple-beet-carrot mixture. Serve at once or chill to serve.

TARRAGON SALAD DRESSING

While this recipe calls for olive oil – because we think it gives a special flavour to the dressing – any other oil may be substituted, including sunflower, corn, or vegetable.
    Serves 6 to 8.

3/4 teaspoon	dry mustard	4 mL
1/4 cup	wine vinegar	50 mL
1/2 cup	olive oil	125 mL

1 tablespoon	soy sauce	15 mL
½ teaspoon	salt	2 mL
½	clove garlic, finely chopped	½
1 teaspoon	fresh OR dried tarragon	5 mL

1. In a small bowl, mix mustard with vinegar; add oil and mix well. Add all remaining ingredients. Mix thoroughly. Refrigerate for later use.

RED PEPPER AND BLUEBERRY SALAD

This is an extraordinarily good, extraordinarily colourful salad. We created it to be served at room temperature when it's made, but we find it's even better served cold the next day.

The recipe is straightforward. In advance, though, there are two simple preparatory steps: grilling the peppers and toasting the almonds.

Serves 4 very originally.

3	large red peppers	3
4 tablespoons	olive oil	60 mL
3 tablespoons	blanched, sliced almonds	45 mL
1 tablespoon	wine vinegar	15 mL
½	clove garlic, finely chopped	½
¼ teaspoon	salt	1 mL
	Freshly ground pepper	
3 tablespoons	blueberries	45 mL
1 tablespoon	finely chopped parsley	15 mL

1. Preheat broiler.
2. Coat peppers with 1 tablespoon (15 mL) oil and broil on all sides until skin is brown and flesh is soft.
3. While peppers are still hot, remove skins. Cut peppers in half lengthwise; remove seeds. Cut peppers lengthwise into strips about ¼ inch (0.75 cm) wide.
4. Preheat oven to 400°F (200°C).
5. Place almonds on cookie sheet. Toast 4 minutes, remove from oven and let cool.
6. In a bowl, mix together remaining oil, vinegar, garlic and salt and pepper to taste.
7. Add blueberries, parsley, and pepper strips. Toss gently, taking care not to bruise or break berries.
8. Sprinkle with toasted almonds.

MARINATED CAULIFLOWER SALAD WITH TARRAGON

A delightful dish that can be served as an hors d'oeuvre to party guests or to family at the dinner table.
Serves 4.

1	cauliflower, trimmed and separated into flowerets	1

MARINADE:

⅓ cup	oil	75 mL
2 tablespoons	wine vinegar	30 mL
½ teaspoon	salt	2 mL
	Freshly ground pepper	
1 teaspoon	Dijon mustard	5 mL
1 teaspoon	finely chopped tarragon	5 mL
1 tablespoon	finely chopped onion	15 mL
1	hard-boiled egg, finely chopped	1

1. Drop cauliflower in boiling, salted water to cover and cook, uncovered, until tender but still crisp, 5 to 8 minutes. Drain. Rinse under cold running water. Drain and place in serving dish.
2. To make marinade, combine all marinade ingredients except egg. Mix well. Pour over cauliflower.
3. Marinate at least 3 hours, refrigerated, before serving. Sprinkle with chopped egg. Serve chilled or at room temperature.

YAM AND CHIVE SALAD

An original dish created for The Best of Canada.
Serves 2 to 4.

3	yams, peeled, diced into ¹/₂-inch (1.5-cm) cubes	3
2 tablespoons	sour cream	30 mL
2 teaspoons	chopped chives	10 mL
1 teaspoon	finely chopped ginger root	5 mL
¹/₂ teaspoon	salt	2 mL
	Freshly ground pepper	

1. Place yams in saucepan and cover with cold, salted water. Bring to boil; reduce heat to medium and boil slowly, about 10 minutes or until yams are tender but still firm. Drain. Transfer yams to serving dish.
2. In a separate bowl, mix together sour cream, chives, ginger, salt, and pepper. Pour sauce over yams and toss gently. Serve at once or refrigerate for later serving.

ATLANTIC BABY SHRIMP SALAD

You will find baby shrimp on both the east and west coasts, and they're both delicious.
This salad can be made in advance and refrigerated.
Serves 2.

6 ounces	cooked and frozen Atlantic baby shrimp, thawed and peeled	180 g
¹/₂ cup	finely sliced celery	125 mL
2	scallions (green onions), finely sliced	2
3 tablespoons	sour cream	45 mL
¹/₂ teaspoon	salt	2 mL
	Freshly ground pepper	
¹/₂ teaspoon	Worcestershire sauce	2 mL
1 teaspoon	lemon juice	5 mL
6	Boston lettuce leaves	6
1 tablespoon	chopped fresh dill	15 mL

1. In a bowl, combine first 8 ingredients. Mix thoroughly. Refrigerate until required.
2. To serve, arrange 3 lettuce leaves on each plate; top with shrimp salad. Sprinkle with dill.

ELEGANT CANADIAN
CRAB MEAT SALAD

This crab meat salad, heightened with port, is elegant in itself; but we felt the dish warranted special status because of the elegant serving method that follows the recipe. Hence the name.

While this dish can be made with Alaska king crab, we prefer using the best of Canada; thus our preference for frozen queen crab from the Maritimes.

Queen crab comes cooked and frozen in 1-pound (450-g) bags. It is generally available in three portions: body meat, a combo-pack (which includes body meat and some leg meat), and all leg meat.

For this recipe, the combo-pack is adequate. Do not rinse thawed crab meat; simply squeeze out excess moisture. You may wish to save the crab juice for any seafood sauces you might prepare.

Serves 4.

1 pound	**frozen queen crab meat, thawed**	**450 g**

SAUCE:

1 tablespoon	**finely chopped chives OR onion**	**15 mL**
1 teaspoon	**curry powder**	**5 mL**
½ teaspoon	**Dijon mustard**	**2 mL**
½ teaspoon	**prepared horseradish**	**2 mL**
1 teaspoon	**light soy sauce**	**5 mL**
1 teaspoon	**finely chopped tarragon**	**5 mL**
1 teaspoon	**ketchup**	**5 mL**
¼ teaspoon	**salt**	**1 mL**
⅛ teaspoon	**freshly ground pepper**	**0.5 mL**
5 teaspoons	**Canadian port**	**25 mL**
3 tablespoons	**yogurt**	**45 mL**

SERVING SUGGESTION:

	Lettuce leaves	
2 tablespoons	**sliced toasted almonds**	**30 mL**
1	**cantaloupe**	**1**
2	**grapefruit**	**2**

1. Shred the crab meat, or cut into pieces less than ½ inch (1.5 cm) long.
2. Combine all 11 sauce ingredients; mix well. Add crab meat. Toss. Refrigerate and serve in one of the following ways: Mound salad on lettuce leaves and sprinkle with almonds.

3. For a more elegant presentation, serve in cantaloupe rings; cut ends off melon and discard. Slice melon into 4 circular bands of equal width. Or if cantaloupe is extremely large, slice off 4 bands each 1 inch (2.5 cm) thick and use remaining melon for fruit salad.
4. Remove seeds from core of each band. Lay each slice flat on an individual plate. Using a knife, make 1 continuous cut, separating rind from pulp, but do not cut through rind at any point and do not remove it.
5. Cut pulp within separate (but still adjacent) rind into 8 or 10 sections. Again, do not cut through exterior skin.
6. Peel grapefruit and trim white membrane; carefully separate each into natural sections. Cut each section in half lengthwise.
7. Ring each melon slice with halved grapefruit sections, creating a scalloped edge around melon slice.
8. Mound centre of cantaloupe with crab meat salad. Sprinkle with toasted almonds. Refrigerate until serving.

CELERY ROOT SALAD
WITH YOGURT AND TARRAGON

Celery root, or celeriac, is a large, lumpy vegetable related to common celery. The thick brown turnip-like root has an identifiable celery-like taste.

Serves 2.

1 tablespoon	golden seedless raisins	15 mL
½ teaspoon	Triple Sec liqueur	2 mL
1	large celery root	1
3 tablespoons	yogurt	45 mL
¼ teaspoon	chopped fresh or dried tarragon	1 mL
	Salt and freshly ground pepper	

1. Soak raisins in liqueur for 15 minutes.
2. While raisins are soaking, prepare celery root. Cut bottom and green tops from root and discard. Wash and peel bulb to expose white interior.
3. Cut celery root into julienne strips. There should be about 3 cups.
4. In a bowl, mix together yogurt and tarragon, and season with salt and pepper to taste. Add raisins and any unabsorbed liqueur. Toss with celery root and serve at once.

SPICY CUCUMBER SALAD
WITH YOGURT

This is a Canadianized version of what in India is called raita – a racy yet refreshing accompaniment to spicy dishes.

While this recipe makes enough for 3 to 4, we prefer to make it up by the batchful – in multiples of this recipe – and let it get good and curried in the refrigerator for a day or two.

You might want to try adding half an onion, finely chopped.

Yield: 3 cups (750 mL).

¼ cup	yogurt	50 mL
1 teaspoon	salt	5 mL
1 teaspoon	curry powder	5 mL
2 teaspoons	finely chopped fresh OR dried coriander	10 mL
1	English cucumber, peeled	1
1	tomato, peeled, seeded, diced	1

1. In a bowl, mix together yogurt, salt, curry powder, and coriander.
2. Cut cucumber in half lengthwise. Using tip of spoon, scoop out seeds. Cut in half again lengthwise and thinly slice.
3. Add cucumber and tomato to yogurt mixture. Mix well. Refrigerate.

CRISP SLEEK LEEK SALAD

Here's an unusual way to eat leeks – raw.

Serves 2.

1	medium-sized leek, white and light green portion only	1
1 tablespoon	coarsely chopped parsley	15 mL
¼ cup	Tarragon Salad Dressing (page 166)	50 mL

1. Cut leek lengthwise to within ½ inch (1.5 cm) of bulb end; do not separate halves. Rinse well under running water to remove all sand.
2. Soak leek in cold water for 20 minutes to freshen and make crisp for cutting.
3. Slice leek finely. Add parsley. Toss. Coat with tarragon dressing. Mix well. Serve at room temperature or slightly chilled.

EASY EGGPLANT SALAD

There's nothing worse than a pallid salad. Good salads should have taste, texture, and colour. This one has all three.
Serves 2 to 4.

2	medium-sized eggplants	2
1 tablespoon	oil	15 mL
1	onion, *not* peeled	1
1	clove garlic, finely chopped	1
1 tablespoon	finely chopped mint	15 mL
1	tomato, peeled, seeded, diced	1
½ cup	Tarragon Salad Dressing (page 166)	125 mL

1. Preheat oven to 400°F (200°C).
2. Coat eggplants with oil. Place on baking sheet and bake 15 minutes.
3. Then add onion to baking sheet and bake an additional 30 minutes.
4. Remove vegetables from oven. Let cool. Peel and dice eggplants and onion into ½-inch (1.5-cm) cubes.
5. In a bowl, combine cooked vegetables, garlic, mint, and tomato.
6. Coat with tarragon dressing or your favourite oil and vinegar dressing. Toss and refrigerate until serving.

FREDERICTON FETTUCCINE SALAD

This is a fabulous, original cold seafood pasta salad that can be served in summer or winter. The sauce was created specifically for this dish, but you may also use our Green Sauce (page 220) to coat the noodles.
Serves 6 to 8.

1 cup	julienne sticks of celery (method below)	250 mL
½ cup	julienne sticks of onion (method below)	125 mL
1 ½ cups	julienne sticks of carrot (method below)	375 mL
24	large mussels, scrubbed and debearded (page 64)	24
½ teaspoon	freshly ground pepper	2 mL
2 tablespoons	Canadian sherry	2 mL
1 pound	spinach fettuccine	450 g
SAUCE:		
⅓ cup	mayonnaise	75 mL
1 tablespoon	finely chopped fresh basil OR 1 teaspoon (5 mL) dried	15 mL
1 teaspoon	mustard seeds	5 mL
1	clove garlic, finely chopped	1
1 tablespoon	vinegar	15 mL
1 teaspoon	salt	5 mL
	Freshly ground pepper	

1. Cut celery stalks into 1½-inch (4-cm) lengths. Cut pieces lengthwise into thin sticks.
2. Cut off and discard top and bottom of onion. Cut lengthwise into thin sticks.
3. Cut carrot into pieces 1½ inches (4 cm) long; cut pieces lengthwise into thin sticks.
4. In a saucepan over high heat, combine celery, onion, carrot, mussels, pepper and sherry. Cook, covered, 7 minutes, or until mussels open. Drain. Remove mussels from shells, and set meat aside. Set aside vegetable sticks.

5. To prepare pasta, cook noodles in a large pot of boiling, salted water until *al dente*. Drain. Rinse under cold running water until completely cooled, to stop cooking. Drain. Cut noodles into pieces 2 inches (5 cm) long. Set aside.
6. To make sauce, combine all ingredients and mix thoroughly.
7. Combine noodles, mussels, and vegetables. Cover with sauce. Toss. Refrigerate before serving.

ONION, ORANGE, AND BEET SALAD

During the course of creating our fabulous Seven-Day Turkey Feast (pages 125-137), Tony decided one of the turkey dishes cried out for a colourful side salad. We rummaged through the refrigerator and came up with this exotic yet simple dish, as tasty as it is colourful.
Serves 4.

2	oranges	2
3	small beets, boiled until tender	3
1	small purple onion	1
6 tablespoons	olive oil	90 mL
½ teaspoon	Dijon mustard	2 mL
3 tablespoons	tarragon vinegar OR 1 teaspoon (5 mL) tarragon mixed with 3 tablespoons (45 mL) vinegar	45 mL
	Salt and freshly ground pepper	

1. Using a sharp knife, remove peel and all white membrane from oranges. Cut oranges into thin slices crosswise.
2. Peel boiled beets and cut into thin slices crosswise.
3. Similarly, cut onion into thin slices; separate into rings.
4. Prepare dressing by mixing oil and mustard. Add vinegar, salt and pepper to taste; mix well.
5. To arrange salad on individual plates, place orange slices around plates' edges. Arrange beet slices inside circle of oranges. Place onion rings in centre. Sprinkle with dressing.

BEET AND APPLE SALAD

This is a colourful, tasty salad that can be served hot or cold.
Serves 6.

4	large beets	4
1 tablespoon	salt	15 mL
2	cloves	2
2 tablespoons	finely chopped onion	30 mL
2	apples, peeled, quartered, sliced	2
	Freshly ground pepper	
3 tablespoons	olive oil	45 mL
2 tablespoons	vinegar	30 mL
1 tablespoon	soy sauce	15 mL
¼ teaspoon	salt	1 mL

1. Trim beet tops. Drop beets and cloves in boiling, salted water to cover, and cook, uncovered, until tender, about 30 to 60 minutes. Drain and rinse under cold running water to set colour. Drain; rub off skin. When beets are cool, quarter and cut into slices.
2. In a bowl, mix together beets, onion, and apples; pepper to taste.
3. In a separate bowl, mix together oil, vinegar, soy sauce and salt. Pour sauce over beet mixture and toss well. Serve at room temperature or chilled.

TNT SALAD
(TOMATOES 'N' TARRAGON)

Why the TNT Salad? Because the combination of Tomatoes 'n' Tarragon is dynamite. We're crazy for this simple salad. It takes no time to prepare.
   Serves 4.

1 tablespoon	olive oil	15 mL
1½ teaspoons	wine vinegar	7 mL
½ teaspoon	salt	2 mL
¼ teaspoon	freshly ground pepper	1 mL
1	clove garlic, finely chopped	1
1 teaspoon	fresh OR dried tarragon	5 mL
1 pound	cherry tomatoes	450 g

1. Mix together first 6 ingredients. Pour over tomatoes. Toss and serve.

BEANS, CEREALS, CRÊPES, PASTA, AND RICE

THE GREAT CANADIAN CASSOULET

Cassoulet is a famous and traditional bean dish from Languedoc, in southern France. It is made with dried white beans and may contain goose, duck, pork, mutton, or sausage. A hearty, stew-like dish, well seasoned, herbed, and garlicked.

We prefer using cannellini, or white kidney beans, although you can substitute with navy beans or Great Northern beans.

Serves 6 heartily.

2 cups	white kidney beans	500 mL
8 cups	water	2 L
¼ cup	unsalted butter	50 mL
2	partridges, cut in half, bones *not* removed OR 1 duck, cut into serving pieces	2
2	medium-sized onions, coarsely chopped	2
1	bay leaf	1
1	carrot, sliced	1
2	turnips, peeled, quartered, sliced	2
1	head (bulb) garlic, left whole and unpeeled	1
2	tomatoes, peeled, seeded, diced	2
½ teaspoon	rosemary	2 mL
½ teaspoon	thyme	2 mL
1 teaspoon	freshly ground pepper	5 mL
1 tablespoon	salt	15 mL
1	pork hock	1
1	¼-pound (115-g) smoked pork belly, in one piece	1
½ pound	Kielbasa or Polish-style sausage	225 g

1. Soak beans in water for 3 hours. Drain and rinse under cold running water. Drain again. Set aside.
2. In a frying pan over medium heat, melt half the butter. When foam subsides, fry partridges, turning until brown on all sides. Set aside.
3. In a flame-proof casserole or Dutch oven, melt remaining butter over medium heat. When foam subsides, sauté onion and bay leaf until onion is transparent.

4. Add carrot, turnips, garlic, tomatoes, rosemary, thyme, and pepper and continue to sauté 1 additional minute. Stir constantly.
5. Add drained beans, 4 cups (1 L) fresh water, and salt and stir well. Bring to boil. At boil, add partridge pieces, pork hock, pork belly, and sausage. Return to boil.
6. Reduce heat and simmer, covered, 1 hour.
7. Remove partridge pieces and set aside. Continue cooking over low heat, covered, an additional 1/2 hour.
8. Return partridge pieces to casserole. Heat through. Serve.

ROSEMARY'S ELBOW MACARONI

To date, Rosemary's best known affiliation is with a baby; but we think once you've tried this simple-to-make dish, you'll always associate Rosemary with our pasta dish.
Serves 4.

1 pound	elbow macaroni	450 g
1/4 cup	butter	50 mL
2 teaspoons	rosemary	10 mL
1/2 cup	grated medium Canadian Cheddar	125 mL

1. Cook noodles in a large pot of boiling, salted water until *al dente*. Drain.
2. Meanwhile, melt butter in a saucepan over steaming pot of noodles or over medium-low heat. Add drained noodles and thoroughly coat with butter. Add rosemary and cheese. Mix well.
3. Transfer to heated serving dish. Serve with additional grated Cheddar.

THE BEST OF CANADA CRÊPES

Yield: 12 crêpes.

³/₄ cup	all-purpose flour	175 mL
¹/₈ teaspoon	salt	0.5 mL
1	large egg yolk	1
1	large egg, beaten	1
1¹/₄ cups	milk	300 mL
1 tablespoon	unsalted butter, melted	15 mL

1. Sift flour into a bowl. Add salt, egg yolk, and whole beaten egg. Beat well. Add milk, constantly beating with whisk until batter is smooth. Stir in melted butter. Strain batter. Allow to rest at least 1 hour.
2. Place a 5- or 7-inch (13- or 18-cm) skillet or crêpe pan over medium-high heat. When hot, add about 2 teaspoons (10 mL) butter or enough to lightly coat skillet. Use a brush or folded paper towel to spread butter. With a large spoon, add about 3 tablespoons (45 mL) batter to heated skillet. Remove skillet from heat, tilting to spread batter evenly across entire surface. Pour excess batter back into bowl. Return skillet to heat.
3. Cook for a few minutes or until bottom of crêpe is browned and lifts easily from skillet. Flip or turn with spatula, and cook other side for additional few minutes. Remove crêpe and set aside; prepare skillet with additional butter and repeat method until all batter is used.
4. Crêpes may be made in advance, even stacked and frozen with alternating layers of waxed paper or foil.

CAROL'S CRUNCHY GRANOLA

This is it – the best-ever Crunchy Granola. Throw out your boxes of dried breakfast cereals and forget whatever other recipes you've clipped for granola. This is it!

Carol, my wife, devised this recipe through trial and not too much error.

The secret for making any good granola is the honey. In our home, we only use buckwheat honey, which adds a distinctive flavour to the cereal.

Another tip: add the raisins after you've cooked the granola. If you bake the raisins, they will dry out and get hard.

Yield: 10 cups (2.5 L).

²/₃ cup	buckwheat honey	150 mL
½ cup	safflower OR soy oil	125 mL
2 teaspoons	vanilla	10 mL
1 cup	hulled sunflower seeds	250 mL
1 cup	chopped or split cashews	250 mL
2 cups	rolled oats	500 mL
2 cups	wheat flakes	500 mL
1 cup	wheat germ	250 mL
1 cup	shredded coconut	250 mL
½ cup	sesame seeds	125 mL
1 cup	raisins	250 mL

1. Preheat oven to 350°F (180°C).
2. In a saucepan over low heat, combine honey, oil, and vanilla. When honey melts and becomes runny, stir and remove from heat.
3. In a large bowl, combine all other ingredients except raisins. Mix well. Sprinkle with heated honey mixture and toss until all ingredients are coated and sticky.
4. Spread mixture on an oiled baking sheet or in a shallow pan. Bake 25 to 30 minutes, stirring mixture twice during cooking period. Remove and cool. Add raisins. Store in air-tight container.
5. Serve with banana, strawberries, peaches, or any other seasonal fresh fruit, and milk.

NEW BRUNSWICK FETTUCCINE
(GREEN PASTA WITH MUSSELS)

Sorrel is a wonderful, leafy green that resembles romaine in looks, but has a distinctive sour taste. The leaf has been aptly named: sorrel means "sour grass."

In some parts of Canada, pasta makers turn out green fettuccine noodles using sorrel instead of the more customary spinach. Our seafood sauce is a perfect accompaniment to these sorrel noodles, but works in perfect harmony with spinach noodles, too.

This sauce calls for pink peppercorns, which can be found in small, brine-packed jars in specialty stores. If unavailable, substitute with green peppercorns, or regular black peppercorns.

Serves 2.

SAUCE:

½ cup	dry white wine	125 mL
1 tablespoon	chopped fresh parsley	15 mL
1 teaspoon	oregano	5 mL
1 tablespoon	chopped fresh basil OR 1 teaspoon (5 mL) dried	15 mL
1	bay leaf	1
1 teaspoon	pink peppercorns	5 mL
3	cloves garlic, finely chopped	3
24	mussels, scrubbed, debearded (page 64)	24
¼ cup	heavy (35%) cream	50 mL
¼ cup	plain yogurt	50 mL
½ cup	grated medium Canadian Cheddar	125 mL

PASTA:

12 ounces	fettuccine noodles	340 g
¼ cup	butter	50 mL

1. To make sauce: In a sauté pan, combine wine, parsley, oregano, basil, bay leaf, peppercorns, garlic, and mussels. Bring to boil, cover, and steam until all mussels open, about 5 minutes.
2. Remove mussels from shells and set meat aside. Over medium-high heat, reduce liquid to half. Add cream and yogurt and reduce liquid to half again. Remove bay leaf.

3. Add half the grated Cheddar. Mix cheese into the sauce well to ensure that it melts evenly. Set aside, keeping warm.
4. To prepare the pasta: Add noodles to a large pot of boiling salted water. Cook about 12 to 14 minutes, or until tender but still firm.
5. As noodles cook, melt butter in a saucepan over the steaming noodle saucepan. (This is an easy way to melt butter. The steam won't burn the butter, and an extra burner isn't needed.)
6. Drain noodles and add to melted butter, tossing with forks to coat evenly. Add half the heated sauce, mixing thoroughly. Arrange noodles on serving platter; place mussels around edge of platter and cover with remaining sauce.
7. Garnish with remaining grated Cheddar.

LEMON AND PARSLEY RICE

Serves 4.

3 cups	chicken stock	750 mL
½	onion, finely chopped	½
2	cloves garlic, finely chopped	2
½ cup	chopped fresh parsley	125 mL
1	bay leaf	1
	Juice of 1 lemon	
1 teaspoon	salt	5 mL
¼ teaspoon	freshly ground pepper	1 mL
1 cup	long-grain white rice	250 mL
1 tablespoon	unsalted butter	15 mL
1 teaspoon	finely chopped fresh mint	5 mL

1. In a saucepan, combine first 8 ingredients and bring to boil.
2. Add rice slowly, keeping stock at boil. Reduce heat and simmer, covered, 20 minutes, or until all liquid is absorbed.
3. Before serving, stir in butter and mint.

ALMOND WILD RICE

Wild rice isn't rice at all; it's a member of the grass family. It has a delicate natural flavour. In this recipe, that natural flavour is enhanced with almond.

Serves 4.

½ cup	seedless raisins	125 mL
2 tablespoons	Amaretto liqueur	30 mL
1 cup	wild rice	250 mL
5 cups	water	1.2 L
1 teaspoon	salt	5 mL
1	small onion, peeled, studded with 2 whole cloves	1
2 tablespoons	unsalted butter	30 mL
¼ cup	sliced toasted almonds	50 mL

1. Soak raisins in Amaretto for 2 hours.
2. Wash rice in several baths of cold water and remove any foreign particles. Drain and transfer to a saucepan.
3. Add water, salt, and onion and bring to boil. Reduce heat and simmer, covered, 35 minutes or until rice is tender.
4. Drain and remove onion. Add butter and toss until rice is evenly coated. Add raisins with Amaretto and mix in with fork.
5. Sprinkle with toasted almonds and serve.

NOODLES AND CABBAGE

A very simple, very tasty recipe that my mother, Anne, has been making since I was a kid. A Hungarian dish in origin, this may have been my earliest brush with pasta.
Serves 4 to 6.

½ cup	unsalted butter	125 mL
1	medium-sized cabbage, shredded	1
1 teaspoon	sugar	5 mL
2-3 tablespoons	water	30-45 mL
1	12-ounce (340-g) package broad egg noodles	1
	Salt and freshly ground pepper	

1. In a saucepan over medium heat, melt half the butter. Add cabbage and sugar, and sauté, stirring, until cabbage is lightly browned. Add water, cover, and reduce heat to low. Steam cabbage about 5 minutes, or until completely wilted. Remove from heat and set aside.
2. Meanwhile, cook noodles in a large pot of boiling salted water according to package instructions, keeping noodles *al dente*. Drain.
3. Combine noodles and cabbage and add remaining butter. Toss well. Salt and pepper to taste. Serve at once or reheat as required.

RICE PILAF

Tony says the test of a well-cooked rice is to spill it on the table. If it is properly cooked, all the grains will fall individually. While such a test may be the sign of a genius cook, it does nothing to improve waiter relations at the table.

For this recipe, long-grain white rice is preferred. The dish is a perfect accompaniment to chicken, veal, fish, and shellfish.

To add a twist to plain rice: sauté one cup (250 mL) of chopped mushrooms in 2 tablespoons (30 mL) butter and add them to the rice when you add the chicken broth. Or you may want to add a distinctive Italian taste to the dish: mix 1 tablespoon (15 mL) butter with the plain rice and then add ½ cup (125 mL) grated Parmesan cheese just before serving.

Serves 4.

3 tablespoons	unsalted butter	45 mL
½ cup	finely chopped onion	125 mL
1 cup	long-grain white rice	250 mL
½ teaspoon	salt	2 mL
2 cups	chicken stock	500 mL

1. In an ovenproof and flameproof casserole, melt butter over medium heat. When foam subsides, sauté onion until soft and transparent, about 5 minutes.
2. Add rice, stirring constantly until evenly coated with butter. Cook about 1 minute.
3. Add salt and chicken stock. Bring to boil, reduce heat and simmer, covered, 18 to 20 minutes or until all liquid is absored; OR preheat oven to 350°F (180°C), and bake, covered, 18 minutes. Remove from heat.
4. To keep rice heated until served, transfer cooked rice to a second, cooled casserole. Place in a warm oven until serving.

CONFECTIONS
AND DESSERTS

BLUEBERRY RIVER BLUEBERRY BREAD

Blueberry River is in British Columbia. To the people who live in the area we dedicate this recipe. It's an easy one to make and yet a difficult one to beat, especially if you use buckwheat honey. It adds a distinctive taste that clover honey can't match.

Many people ask why the blueberries are coated with flour before they're mixed into the bread. The answer is simple: flour adds a bit of drag and keeps the berries from falling to the bottom of the dough mixture.

Yield: 1 loaf (about 12 slices).

½ cup	unsalted butter	125 mL
½ cup	buckwheat honey	125 mL
2	eggs	2
	Grated zest of 1 lemon	
½ teaspoon	allspice	2 mL
1 teaspoon	cinnamon	5 mL
½ cup	plain 2% yogurt	125 mL
2 cups	whole-wheat flour	500 mL
3 ½ teaspoons	baking powder	17 mL
½ teaspoon	baking soda	2 mL
½ cup	chopped walnuts	125 mL
1 cup	blueberries, coated with 2 tablespoons (30 mL) flour	250 mL

1. Preheat oven to 375°F (190°C).
2. In a bowl, cream together butter and honey until smooth. Add eggs, one at a time, beating constantly.
3. Add grated lemon zest, allspice, and cinnamon. Mix thoroughly.
4. Add yogurt and mix well.
5. In a separate bowl, sift together flour, baking powder, and baking soda. Gradually beat into egg mixture.
6. Fold in walnuts and blueberries.
7. Pour batter into well-buttered, standard (9 × 5 × 3-inch or 1.7-L) loaf pan. Bake 50 to 60 minutes, or until cake tester inserted into bread comes out clean.

WHOLE-WHEAT HEALTH BREAD

When you want to get away from the sugared cinnamon buns, the donuts, and the white bread, try The Best of Canada Whole-Wheat Health Bread. It not only tastes good, it tastes as though it's doing something good for you – which it is.

Yield: 2 loaves.

2	packages dry yeast	2
½ cup	warm water	125 mL
1 cup	quick cooking (*not* instant) oats	250 mL
2 tablespoons	melted butter	30 mL
1 cup	pitted dates, finely chopped	250 mL
2 cups	bran	500 mL
½ cup	raisins	125 mL
2⅔ cups	scalded 2% milk	650 mL
2 teaspoons	salt	10 mL
5 ½ cups	whole-wheat flour	1.3 L

1. In a small bowl, dissolve yeast in warm water and let stand 5 minutes.
2. In a separate bowl, combine oats, butter, dates, bran, raisins, milk, and salt, blending thoroughly. Let mixture cool to lukewarm. Add dissolved yeast. Mix well.
3. Gradually add flour, beating until a soft dough forms. Knead until elastic on a well-floured surface.
4. Place dough in greased bowl, turning to coat all surfaces. Cover and let rise in warm place for about 1 hour, or until doubled in bulk.
5. Punch dough down and shape into 2 loaves. Place each loaf in a well-greased 9 × 5 × 3-inch (2-L) loaf pan, cover and let rise again in a warm place until almost double in bulk, about 45 minutes.
6. Preheat oven to 350°F (180°C). Bake loaves 1 hour. Remove from loaf pans and cool on racks.

NORTHERN SPY APPLE CAKE

Northern Spy apples make some of the very best baked apple desserts, as this recipe will attest.

In some years, the Northern Spy apple is harvested early enough to enable you to make this cake for Thanksgiving; if you do, your guests will be giving you thanks. But if Northern Spies are not available, substitute with Greening or Cortland apples – both are filled with good natural acidity.

Serves 8 to 10.

1½ cups	corn oil	375 mL
2 cups	brown sugar, firmly packed	500 mL
3	large eggs	3
3 cups	unsifted cake and pastry flour	750 mL
1 teaspoon	baking powder	5 mL
1 teaspoon	baking soda	5 mL
½ teaspoon	salt	2 mL
	Peel from 1 lemon, grated	
2 teaspoons	cinnamon	10 mL
3 cups	diced unpeeled Northern Spy apples	750 mL
½ cup	chopped walnuts	125 mL
¾ cup	raisins	175 mL

1. Preheat oven to 350°F (180°C).
2. Grease and flour a 10-inch diameter (2.5-L) tube pan.
3. In a bowl, using an electric beater, beat oil and sugar for 2 minutes.
4. Add eggs, one at a time, and continue beating.
5. In a separate bowl, combine flour, baking powder, baking soda, and salt. Mix well. Add dry ingredients to egg-sugar mixture, beating continuously.
6. Add grated lemon peel, cinnamon, apples, walnuts, and raisins. Mix with wooden spoon until blended.
7. Spoon batter into tube pan. Smooth top. Bake 1½ hours or until cake is done.

SUTTON PLACE AMARETTO CHEESECAKE

There are desserts and there are desserts – and then there's Tony's Amaretto Cheesecake, which is in a class by itself. It put Sutton Place in Toronto on the dessert circuit of serious calorie addicts. One piece is never enough.

What makes the cheesecake particularly good are amaretti, or almond macaroons, crushed for the crust. Many amaretti cookies found in the supermarketplace are made with a peanut base and flavoured with almond extract. The search for real amaretti has its own reward: dessert Nirvana.
Serves 8.

CRUST:		
3 cups	crushed *amaretti* (almond macaroons)	750 mL
½ cup	unsalted butter	125 mL

FILLING:		
2¼ pounds	cream cheese, softened	1 kg
⅓ cup	sugar	75 mL
¼ teaspoon	vanilla	1 mL
¼ cup	Amaretto liqueur OR ½ cup (125 mL) Brights Cremeretto sherry	50 mL
4	eggs	4
¾ cup	sour cream	175 mL

1. Preheat oven to 325°F (165°C).
2. To make crust, crush amaretti biscuits into fine crumbs in a food processor fitted with steel blade, or in a blender. Melt butter over low heat and sprinkle over crumbs. Blend well.
3. Press crumbs onto sides and bottom of well-buttered 9-inch (2.5-L) springform pan. Bake 10 minutes; cool.
4. Increase oven setting to 350°F (180°C).
5. To make filling: blend together cream cheese and sugar. Beat until creamy, using an electric mixer.
6. Add vanilla and Amaretto. Add eggs one at a time. Continue beating until mixture is uniformly smooth.
7. Fill crust-lined springform pan with cream cheese mixture. Bake 1 hour. Remove from oven. Top with sour cream. Use spatula to spread sour cream evenly. Return to oven and bake an additional ½ hour.
8. Remove from oven. Let cool. Refrigerate overnight before unmoulding.

MARGARITH'S HAZELNUT COFFEE RING

Tony's wife, Margarith, created this tasty pastry for him; now it bears her name. Tony's trying to convince Margarith that she ought to make it regularly; it's too good to go long periods of time without. Which may not be great English, but it's great cake.

Serves 16.

DOUGH:

1½	envelopes dry yeast	1 ½
½ cup	warm whole milk	125 mL
⅓ cup	sugar	75 mL
3½ cups	all-purpose flour	875 mL
⅔ cup	butter, melted	150 mL
1	large egg, beaten	1
	Grated peel of 1 lemon	
	Pinch of salt	
2 tablespoons	butter, melted	30 mL

FILLING:

2	large eggs, beaten	2
⅔ cup	sugar	150 mL
2 cups	ground hazelnuts	500 mL
	Juice and peel of ½ lemon	

GLAZE:

¾ cup	icing sugar	175 mL
1 tablespoon	hot water	15 mL
1 tablespoon	dark Canadian rum	15 mL

1. To make dough, dissolve yeast in warm milk with 1 teaspoon (5 mL) sugar. Let stand 5 minutes.
2. Sift flour into large bowl. Make well in centre of flour and pour in dissolved yeast-milk mixture. Mix, incorporating flour, small amounts at a time. When flour is thoroughly mixed, cover bowl with warm, damp towel and let stand 10 minutes.
3. Remove towel and add melted butter, remaining sugar, egg, lemon peel, and salt. Mix well and knead on well-floured surface until dough is smooth and elastic. Place in bowl, cover and let rise in warm place for about 1 hour, or until dough doubles in bulk.

4. On a well-floured surface, roll dough out and make a rectangle about 23 × 17 inches (58 × 43 cm). Brush surface of rectangle with melted butter.
5. To make filling, combine all ingredients. Mix well. Spread filling mixture evenly over buttered sheet of dough.
6. Roll up dough from long side, working away from you. Shape into ring and place in well-buttered 9-inch (2.3-L) ring mould. Cover and let rise in a warm place for about 45 minutes, or until dough has doubled in bulk.
7. Preheat oven to 375°F (190°C).
8. Bake ring 30 minutes, or until golden.
9. To make glaze, mix together all ingredients. Brush on ring while still warm. Let cool.

WORLD'S EASIEST CHEESECAKE

Tony's Amaretto Cheesecake may be the world's tastiest, but this has got to be the easiest, and the flavour is divine. This recipe came into family use many years ago through friends. Serves 8.

3	8-ounce (225-g) packages cream cheese, softened	3
6	eggs	6
1⅓ cups	sugar	325 mL
2 cups	sour cream	500 mL
2 teaspoons	vanilla	10 mL

1. Preheat oven to 325°F (165°C).
2. In a bowl, beat cream cheese until light and creamy. Add eggs, one at a time, beating continuously until smooth.
3. Fold in 1 cup (250 mL) sugar. Pour mixture into well-greased 10-inch (2.8-L) springform pan. Bake 50 minutes. Let cool 20 minutes.
4. Meanwhile, blend together sour cream, remaining sugar, and vanilla. Spoon mixture over cooled cheesecake. Return to oven and bake an additional 15 minutes.
5. Remove from oven. Cool. Refrigerate.
6. To serve, garnish with crushed pineapple, frozen raspberries, or any fresh, seasonal fruit.

NIAGARA PEACH ROLL

A peachy dessert for summer entertaining, this can be made in the morning for an evening dinner.
Serves 10 to 12.

CAKE:

4	eggs, separated	4
1/3 cup	sugar	75 mL
1/4 cup	cake and pastry flour	50 mL
1/4 cup	cornstarch	50 mL
1 teaspoon	vanilla	5 mL
1 teaspoon	grated lemon rind	5 mL

FILLING:

1/3 cup	sliced, peeled peaches, fresh OR canned	75 mL
1/3 cup	peach OR apricot marmalade	75 mL
1/2 teaspoon	cornstarch	2 mL
1/4 cup	peach juice OR water	50 mL
2/3 cup	heavy (35%) cream	150 mL
3/4 cup	chopped walnuts	175 mL

TOPPING:

2 tablespoons	Meagher's peach brandy	30 mL
2 tablespoons	icing sugar	30 mL

1. Preheat oven to 400°F (200°C).
2. To prepare cake, butter a standard-sized jelly-roll pan (10 1/2 × 15 1/2 × 1 inch [2 L]), line with waxed paper, and butter the paper.
3. Using an electric mixer, beat egg yolks in a bowl with sugar until mixture forms a ribbon when beater is lifted.
4. In separate bowl, beat egg whites until stiff. Fold whites gently into yolk mixture.
5. Sift together flour and cornstarch and stir into egg mixture; stir in vanilla and grated lemon rind.
6. Spread batter evenly into jelly-roll pan. Bake 10 minutes, or until lightly golden. Remove from oven. Cover cake with dampened dish towel and invert onto towel. Carefully peel waxed paper off cake. Let cake cool.
7. To make filling, purée peach slices and marmalade in a blender. Transfer purée to saucepan and bring to boil.

8. Meanwhile, dissolve cornstarch in peach juice. Add to boiling purée. Bring back to boil, then remove from heat. Set aside to cool.
9. In a separate bowl, whip cream and fold into cooled peach purée. Fold in walnuts.
10. To prepare peach roll, sprinkle cooled cake with peach brandy. Cover evenly with peach-whipped cream mixture. Roll cake up from long side, producing roll approximately 15 inches (38.5 cm) long.
11. Sprinkle roll with icing sugar. Refrigerate before serving.

PERFECT POUND CAKE

You can buy pound cake in the supermarket, but nothing makes our Niagara Falls Trifle (page 208) or Rocky Mountain Raspberry Cake (page 200) taste better than homemade pound cake.

This recipe makes enough for either dessert recipe.

Yield: 1 loaf.

²/₃ cup	soft unsalted butter	150 mL
1 cup	sugar	250 mL
3	eggs	3
1 teaspoon	vanilla	5 mL
	Grated peel of 1 lemon	
1 teaspoon	salt	5 mL
2 cups	cake and pastry flour	500 mL
½ teaspoon	double-acting baking powder	2 mL
²/₃ cup	milk	150 mL

1. Preheat oven to 300°F (150°C).
2. In a bowl, cream together butter and sugar.
3. Beat in eggs, one at a time. Add vanilla, grated lemon peel, and salt. Mix well.
4. Sift together flour and baking powder and gradually beat into butter-egg mixture alternately with milk, beginning and ending with dry ingredients.
5. Pour batter into a well-greased 9 × 5-inch (1.7-L) loaf pan.
6. Bake 1 ¼ hours or until done.

THE GREAT CANADIAN
MARBLE STRAWBERRY CAKE

Nearly as long as the method that follows – that's how long guests will be talking about your Great Canadian Marble Cake, made with summer's sweetest berries. But don't be put off; the recipe looks long but is relatively simple.

We call this a marble cake because when you cut into it, the layers of cream, berries, and cake resemble a piece of Italian marble.

Serves 8 to 10.

WHITE SPONGE:

7	eggs	7
¾ cup	sugar	175 mL
¾ cup	cake and pastry flour	175 mL

1. Preheat oven to 350°F (180°C).
2. Using an electric mixer or food processor fitted with steel blade, beat eggs and sugar about 5 minutes, or until mixture is pale and foamy.
3. Add flour gradually, blending thoroughly.
4. Pour into a well-greased 9-inch (1.5-L) round cake pan. Place on middle rack in oven. Bake about 20 minutes. Test for doneness by inserting cake tester or long needle; when cake is done, needle will come out clean. Remove from oven and cool.

BUTTER CREAM: 1ST STAGE

5	egg whites	5
⅔ cup	sugar	150 mL

1. Using an electric mixer, beat egg whites until soft peaks form. Gradually add sugar, and beat until stiff.

2ND STAGE:

1¼ cups	sugar	300 mL
½ cup	water	125 mL

1. Boil water with sugar for 5 minutes. Remove from heat and fold into egg-white mixture above. Stir until mixture is no longer warm.

2 cups	unsalted butter	500 mL
1/4 cup	shortening	50 mL

1. In a bowl, blend together butter and shortening. (The shortening will add a fluffiness to butter cream.) Slowly incorporate butter and shortening into egg-syrup mixture. Mix thoroughly.

ASSEMBLING:

2/3 cup	Brights Cremeretto sherry	150 mL
2/3 cup	maple syrup	150 mL
4-5 cups	strawberries, washed, patted dry, tops removed (about 50 berries)	1 L
1	1-ounce (30-g) square unsweetened chocolate, grated	1

1. Cut sponge cake horizontally into 3 layers, each about 3/4 inch (2 cm) thick. Place 1 layer of cake on a serving platter. This will be the bottom layer of the assembled cake.
2. In a bowl, mix Cremeretto with maple syrup. Sprinkle 7 tablespoons (105 mL) mixture over cake. Cake should be moist but not soggy.
3. Using a spatula, spread a 1/2-inch (1.5-cm) layer of butter cream over cake. For a smooth surface, dip spatula frequently in hot water.
4. Place about 25 strawberries on top of butter cream, laying berries on their sides, tips pointing toward centre. Make one complete circle of berries at cake's outer edge. Start a new circle closer to the centre; line up berries so they lie between the berries of outer row.
5. Cover strawberries with blanket of butter cream.
6. Place second layer of sponge cake over layer of butter cream. Sprinkle with 7 tablespoons (105 mL) Cremeretto-maple syrup mixture. Cover with thin layer of butter cream. Add a second layer of strawberries, again setting berries on their sides with tips pointing toward centre. Cover with blanket of butter cream.
7. Cover with third layer of sponge cake. Sprinkle with remaining Cremeretto-maple syrup mixture. Ice top and sides with remaining butter cream.
8. Decorate with grated chocolate. Cake may be served at room temperature or slightly chilled.

ROCKY MOUNTAIN RASPBERRY CAKE

A delicious, original dessert, best made with fresh raspberries.

Serves 6 to 8.

1	pound cake (page 197), cut into slices ½ inch (1.5 cm) thick	1
2 tablespoons	maple syrup	30 mL
¼ cup	raspberry sauce (page 216)	50 mL
2 tablespoons	Brights Cremeretto sherry	30 mL
1 cup	fresh raspberries OR 1 9-ounce (255-g) package frozen raspberries	250 mL
2 teaspoons	sugar	10 mL
1 cup	heavy (35%) cream	250 mL

1. Line bottom of 9-inch (1-L) pie plate with slices of pound cake.
2. Mix together maple syrup, raspberry sauce, and Cremeretto. Sprinkle over pound cake.
3. Cover with raspberries. Sprinkle with sugar.
4. In a separate bowl, beat cream until stiff peaks form. Spoon over raspberries and spread with spatula to cover all fruit and cake. Serve immediately, or chill before serving.

SPAGHETTI SQUASH MARMALADE

Spaghetti squash is a stubby member of the squash family. When cooked, its fleshy interior unravels into string-like filaments – thus the name.

Yield: 6 cups (1.5 L).

3 pounds	spaghetti squash, peeled, halved, seeded, cut into 1-inch (2.5-cm) cubes	1.3 kg
6 cups	sugar	1.5 L
2	lemons, quartered lengthwise, cut crosswise into thin slices	2
1 tablespoon	crystallized ginger (page 222)	15 mL

1. In a saucepan, combine squash, sugar, lemon, and ginger. Bring to a boil. Reduce heat and simmer, uncovered, 1³/₄ hours, stirring occasionally.
2. Fill hot, dry jars to brim with hot marmalade and cover tightly. There is no need to create a vacuum seal, and the marmalade does not have to be refrigerated until opened.

BEST-EVER CHOCOLATE-CHIP COOKIES

A lot of purists insist the best cookies are made with butter. For almost all our cooking we use butter; we don't use margarine for cooking, or shortening for baking. But this is an exception. Nothing seems to make better chocolate-chip cookies than vegetable shortening. We've used them all and prefer Crisco.

Yield: 36 C.C.C. (chocolate-chip cookies).

1 cup	shortening	250 mL
³/₄ cup	brown sugar	175 mL
³/₄ cup	white sugar	175 mL
2	large eggs	2
1¹/₂ cups	whole-wheat flour	375 mL
1 teaspoon	baking soda	5 mL
1 teaspoon	salt	5 mL
2 cups	chocolate chips	500 mL
2 cups	quick-cooking oatmeal (*not* instant)	500 mL
1 teaspoon	pure vanilla extract	5 mL
1 cup	chopped walnuts	250 mL

1. Preheat oven to 375°F (190°C).
2. In a bowl, cream together shortening and brown and white sugars. Add eggs and beat well.
3. In a separate bowl, sift together flour, soda, and salt. Add to shortening mixture. Beat. Stir in chocolate chips, oatmeal, vanilla, and walnuts. Blend thoroughly.
4. Drop by the tablespoon onto greased cookie sheet. Bake 8 to 10 minutes. Let cool.

MAPLE LEAF MOUSSE

*This is an extraordinary dessert, testimony to Tony's profes-
sionalism and patriotism. Maple Leaf Mousse is an original
creation for* The Best of Canada, *a celebration of Canada's
maple syrup.*
Serves 8 to 10.

2	envelopes gelatin	2
½ cup	dry white wine	125 mL
½ cup	maple syrup	125 mL
4	eggs, separated	4
¼ cup	brown sugar	50 mL
⅔ cup	Rieder Maple liqueur	150 mL
1 teaspoon	crystallized ginger, finely chopped (page 222)	5 mL
2 cups	heavy (35%) cream	500 mL
1	1-ounce (30-g) square unsweetened chocolate, grated	1

1. Sprinkle gelatin over wine and let soften 5 minutes.
2. Add maple syrup and mix well.
3. In a stainless-steel bowl over simmering water OR in top of double boiler, beat egg yolks 2 to 3 minutes, until thick and a lemon yellow in colour. Beat maple syrup mixture into yolks. Cook, stirring constantly, until mixture thickens enough to coat wooden spoon. Do not boil or eggs will curdle. Remove from heat and let cool.
4. When yolks are cool, add sugar, stirring constantly. Add maple liqueur and ginger. Mix well.
5. In a separate bowl, beat egg whites until stiff.
6. In yet another bowl, beat cream until stiff.
7. When maple gelatin mixture is partially set, fold in whipped cream; then gently fold in egg whites.
8. Meanwhile, rinse a 2-quart (2-L) Charlotte mould (or soufflé mould) in cold water; drain excess water but do not dry. Fill with mousse mixture. (The slight film of cool water will keep mousse from sticking to mould.)
9. Chill mousse for at least 4 hours. To unmould, run knife around edge of mousse, and briefly set bottom of mould in hot water. Garnish with grated chocolate.

APRICOT SOUFFLÉ
À LA NOUVELLE CUISINE

Serves 4.

5	egg whites	5
6 tablespoons	sugar	90 mL
2	egg yolks	2
¼ cup	apricot purée OR jam	50 mL
2 teaspoons	crystallized ginger (page 222), finely chopped	10 mL
	Melted butter	
4	*amaretti* biscuits (almond macaroons) OR 1-inch (2.5-cm) cubes of pound cake (page 197)	4
4 teaspoons	Melchers Kanata liqueur	20 mL
4 teaspoons	praline with ginger (page 211, part of method in Peach Champagne Sabayon)	20 mL

1. Preheat oven to 375°F (190°C).
2. Using an electric mixer, beat egg whites until soft peaks form. Slowly add 3 tablespoons (45 mL) sugar. Beat until stiff peaks form.
3. Add egg yolks and continue beating 1 additional minute.
4. Gently fold apricot purée and crystallized ginger into mixture.
5. Carefully brush four 4-inch (200-mL) ramekins with melted butter, coating bottom and sides. Butter lip especially well, so that soufflé will properly rise.
6. Add 3 tablespoons (45 mL) sugar to first buttered ramekin; shake and turn to fully coat buttered surfaces. Pour loose sugar into second buttered ramekin and repeat dusting procedure; sugar all 4 ramekins in this way and discard any surplus sugar.
7. In each ramekin, place 1 *amaretti* biscuit or 1 cube of pound cake. Sprinkle each with 1 teaspoon Kanata liqueur.
8. Fill ramekins ¾ full with apricot mixture. Set in a baking dish filled with about 1 inch (2.5 cm) water. Bake water-cushioned ramekins 12 to 15 minutes, or until soufflés rise about 2 inches (5 cm) above moulds.
9. Sprinkle each soufflé with 1 teaspoon praline and ginger. Serve at once.

PERSIMMON CHIFFON PIE

A lovely, colourful, and tasty dessert for any holiday meal. Persimmons are available late in the year and any Thanksgiving or Christmas dinner would be perfectly complemented with this pie.

Look for deep-orange persimmons. The fruit should be free of bruises. For this recipe, the persimmons must be absolutely ripe. Unripe persimmons have a slightly bitter taste that can overpower the finished pie.

Yield: One 9-inch (1-L) pie.

	Dough for 9-inch (1-L) pie shell (page 207)	
1¼	envelopes unflavoured gelatin	1 ¼
¼ cup	cool water	50 mL
3	eggs, separated	3
½ cup	sugar	125 mL
	Juice and grated rind of ½ lime	
1 cup	persimmon purée (2 medium-sized persimmons, skin split, pulp spooned out and puréed in food processor)	250 mL
¼ teaspoon	cream of tartar	1 mL
½ cup	heavy (35%) cream, whipped	125 mL

1. Preheat oven to 400°F (200°C). Line a 9-inch (1-L) pie plate with pastry dough. Mould to fit contours, line with foil, and weight down with beans or rice. Bake 10 minutes, or until done. Remove foil and beans or rice and let pie shell cool.
2. In a cup, dissolve gelatin in cool water and let soften 5 minutes.
3. In a stainless-steel bowl over simmering water OR in top of double boiler, beat egg yolks. Add sugar and stir constantly 3 to 4 minutes, or until egg mixture thickens. Do not allow to boil.
4. Add lime juice and dissolved gelatin to mixture. Stir until gelatin is evenly mixed. Remove from heat.
5. Add persimmon purée, stirring well. Let mixture cool until partially set, about 20 minutes.
6. In a bowl, beat egg whites with cream of tartar until stiff.
7. Beat partially set persimmon mixture. Fold egg whites gently into mixture.

8. Gently fold in whipped cream.
9. Transfer mixture to baked pie shell. Sprinkle with grated lime rind. Chill at least 2 hours before serving.

FAVOURITE CANADIAN APPLE PIE

Yield: 9-inch (1-L) pie.

	Dough for 9-inch (1-L) pie shell (page 207)	
1½ cups	ground almonds	375 mL
2	eggs, separated	2
1 teaspoon	cinnamon	5 mL
½ cup	sugar	125 mL
2	large apples, peeled, grated	2
	Juice and grated rind of ½ lemon	
2 tablespoons	bread crumbs	30 mL
6	small apples, peeled	6
¼ cup	crab apple OR apple jelly	50 mL

1. Preheat oven to 400°F (200°C). Line a 9-inch (1-L) pie plate with pastry dough. Mould to fit contours, line with foil and weight down with beans or rice. Bake 10 minutes. Remove foil and beans or rice. Let cool. Keep oven at 400°F (200°C).
2. In a bowl, mix almonds, egg yolks, cinnamon, sugar, grated apple, lemon juice, grated lemon rind, and bread crumbs. Mix thoroughly.
3. Cut small apples in half and core. Place apples cut-side down and make fine cuts about ¾ of the way through apple, about ¼ inch (0.75 cm) apart. Do not slice completely through; do not separate thin slices. Set aside.
4. In a bowl, beat egg whites until stiff. Fold gently into nut-yolk mixture. Pour egg mixture into cooled pie shell. Arrange apple halves over mixture, sliced-side up, gently pressing halves down to fan out. Bake 50 to 60 minutes on middle rack of oven.
5. In a small saucepan, heat jelly. When pie is done, brush with heated jelly. Let cool before cutting.

OTTAWA VALLEY
STRAWBERRY PIE

This recipe works best if you use berries that are ripe, red, and abundant. Knowing, however, that some people's desire for strawberry pie is long and the growing season short, we've adapted our recipe for the frozen variety as well.

Yield: One 9-inch (1-L) pie.

	Dough for 9-inch (1-L) pie shell (page 207)	
1	envelope gelatin	1
¼ cup	cool water	50 mL
3	large eggs, separated	3
¾ cup	sugar	175 mL
2 tablespoons	lemon juice	30 mL
1 cup	crushed frozen strawberries and their juice OR crushed, well-ripened fresh berries	250 mL
3 tablespoons	Kirsch	45 mL
1	large banana, sliced and marinated in lemon juice	1
¼ teaspoon	cream of tartar	1 mL
½ cup	heavy (35%) cream	125 mL
	Fresh strawberries for garnish	

1. Preheat oven to 400°F (200°C). Line a 9-inch (1-L) pie plate with pastry dough. Mould to fit contours. Line with foil and weight down with beans or rice. Bake 10 minutes or until done. Remove foil and beans or rice, and let cool.
2. In a cup, sprinkle gelatin over cool water and let soften 5 minutes.
3. In a stainless-steel bowl over a pot of simmering water OR in top of double boiler, beat egg yolks about 3 minutes. Add ½ cup (125 mL) sugar and 1 tablespoon (15 mL) lemon juice, beating constantly until mixture is thick enough to coat a wooden spoon. Do not bring to boil or eggs will curdle. Stir in dissolved gelatin. Remove from heat.
4. Mix crushed strawberries with Kirsch and add to mixture. Blend well. Let mixture cool until partially set, about 20 minutes.
5. When crust has cooled, line pie shell with banana slices and brush with 1 tablespoon (15 mL) lemon juice.

6. In a separate bowl, beat egg whites until frothy. Add cream of tartar, beating until stiff. Beat in remaining ¼ cup (50 mL) sugar.
7. Beat partially set strawberry mixture.
8. In a separate, chilled bowl, whip cream; fold into strawberry mixture. Gently fold in egg whites.
9. Transfer mixture to pie shell. Top with fresh strawberries. Chill at least 2 hours before serving.

PÂTE BRISÉE:
THE PERFECT PIE CRUST

Also known as a "French short crust," this is a basic pie dough. It is suitable for all recipes in our book that call for pie shells – quiches, tarts, and flans.

A properly made pâte brisée will hold the wettest filling you can devise – even the cream of a quiche – without going soggy.

To make dough for a double-crust fruit pie, double the following recipe. Tony has a twist for the top crust: as he rolls out the dough, just before his last couple of passes with a rolling pin, he dusts the dough with sugar. The sugar disappears into the dough, making the top crust crispier.

You may wish to make multiples of this recipe. Wrapped dough balls will keep in the refrigerator for up to 2 weeks.

Yield: one 9-inch (1-L) pie shell.

1¼ cups	cake and pastry flour	300 mL
⅓ cup	unsalted butter, cold, cut into small pieces	75 mL
2 tablespoons	shortening	30 mL
¼ teaspoon	salt	1 mL
3 tablespoons	iced water	45 mL

1. In a bowl, mix together flour, cold butter pieces, shortening, and salt. Work mixture with fingers and gradually start working with hands.
2. Make a well in centre of coarse mixture; add iced water slowly, stirring into dough mixture with fingers. Shape dough into a ball. Do not overwork. Little bits of butter should be visible, not fully worked into dough. This will give dough a buttery puffiness.
3. Dust ball of dough with flour, wrap in waxed paper, and refrigerate at least 1 hour before using.

NIAGARA FALLS TRIFLE

We call this trifle the Niagara version because everyone who tries it falls in love with it. This dessert can be made a day in advance, making it an excellent choice for parties.

Consider replacing raspberries with whatever fruit is in season: peaches, blueberries, or strawberries.

Serves 10 to 12.

CUSTARD:

4 cups	milk	1 L
6 tablespoons	sugar	90 mL
1 tablespoon	vanilla	15 mL
¼ cup	custard powder dissolved in ½ cup (125 mL) cold milk	50 mL
1 cup	heavy (35%) cream	250 mL

TRIFLE:

1	pound cake (page 197), cut into slices ¼ inch (0.75 cm) thick	1
¾ cup	Brights Cremocha sherry	175 mL
2 tablespoons	raspberry sauce (page 216)	30 mL
½ cup	canned crushed pineapple	125 mL
½ cup	finely chopped pitted dates	125 mL
½ cup	fresh raspberries OR frozen, syrup drained	125 mL
1	banana, thinly sliced	1
2 tablespoons	toasted slivered almonds	30 mL
	Whipped cream to decorate	

1. To make custard: Bring milk to boil in a saucepan. Add sugar and vanilla, stirring well. Reduce heat to medium.
2. Add dissolved custard powder and stir constantly until mixture thickens. Remove from heat and let cool.
3. In a separate bowl, beat cream until stiff. Fold gently into cooled custard. Set aside.
4. To assemble trifle, line bottom of 8-inch (1.7-L) glass bowl with slices of pound cake. Sprinkle with ¼ cup (50 mL) Cremocha. Sprinkle with raspberry sauce. Cover with crushed pineapple. Cover with layer of custard. Sprinkle with dates.
5. Cover with a second layer of pound-cake slices. Sprinkle with ¼ cup (50 mL) Cremocha. Cover with raspberries. Cover with another layer of custard.

6. Cover with a third layer of pound-cake slices. Sprinkle with remaining Cremocha. Cover with banana slices. Sprinkle with almonds. Top with remaining custard.
7. Refrigerate. Before serving, fill a pastry bag with whipped cream and decorate top.

BRANDON BRAN MUFFINS

These are phenomenal muffins. We've made them every conceivable way and still get the tastiest, fluffiest batch when we pour the batter into muffin tins, refrigerate, and let rest 24 hours. Sure, you can bake them if the batter only rests 12 hours; and they're still great even if you bake them right away without resting the batter (though the muffins don't seem to rise as high). In fact, no matter how you treat them, they're still better than any store-bought muffin.
Yield: 36 muffins.

3	large eggs	3
1 cup	brown sugar	250 mL
³/₄ cup	molasses	175 mL
¼ cup	maple syrup	50 mL
½ teaspoon	salt	2 mL
3½ cups	milk	875 mL
1¼ cups	corn oil	300 mL
4 teaspoons	baking powder	20 mL
4 teaspoons	baking soda	20 mL
4 cups	whole-wheat flour	1 L
4 cups	bran	1 L
1 cup	raisins	250 mL
1 cup	pitted dates, finely chopped	250 mL

1. In a bowl, beat eggs using an electric mixer or whisk. Add sugar, molasses, maple syrup, salt, milk, corn oil, baking powder, and baking soda. Mix well.
2. Add flour and bran and blend thoroughly. Stir in raisins and dates.
3. Spoon mixture into well-buttered muffin tins; fill each cup about ³/₄ full. Let mixture rest in moulds, refrigerated, for 24 hours (for optimal results).
4. Preheat oven to 400°F (200°C). Bake 15 to 20 minutes.

PEACH CHAMPAGNE SABAYON

Sabayon is a hot, creamy French dessert; the Italians call it zabaione. The French make theirs with dry white wine; in Italy, it is made with Marsala. We make ours with peaches and Canadian champagne, an original twist and an original recipe for the book.

The recipe's long, but it's long on satisfaction, too. The peaches, sabayon, and praline-ginger can be prepared a day in advance. The sabayon should be assembled the day you want to serve it.

The praline-ginger – an essential ingredient – can be used on cream cakes, chiffon pies, fancy gâteaux, whipped cream desserts, or even as a garnish for ice cream.

Serves 4.

PEACHES:

3 cups	water	750 mL
3 cups	sugar	750 mL
	Juice of ½ lemon	
1 teaspoon	grated lemon rind	5 mL
1	2-inch (5-cm) cinnamon stick	1
2	cloves	2
4	fresh peaches	4

1. In a saucepan, combine water, sugar, and lemon juice. Bring to boil and cook, covered, 4 minutes.
2. Add lemon rind, cinnamon, cloves, and peaches. Reduce heat to medium and cook, covered, an additional 4 minutes, or until peach skins start to peel off.
3. Take peaches out of syrup and remove skins. Cover peaches with cooked syrup while cooling. Set aside. Peaches can be refrigerated until sabayon is to be assembled.

CHAMPAGNE SABAYON:

1	whole egg	1
4	egg yolks	4
½ cup	sugar	125 mL
¼ cup	Canadian port	50 mL
½ cup	Canadian champagne	125 mL
½ cup	heavy (35%) cream	125 mL

1. In a stainless-steel bowl over a pot of simmering water OR in the top of a double boiler, combine whole egg, egg yolks, sugar, and port. Beat constantly in same direction until mixture starts to thicken, about 3 minutes. Do not bring mixture to boil.
2. When mixture is slightly thickened, gradually add champagne in a slow trickle, stirring continuously. Mixture should remain thick and fluffy. It should take about 4 to 5 minutes to work in all the champagne. Do not bring mixture to boil. When champagne is fully absorbed, remove mixture from heat and set aside. At this point, the sabayon can be refrigerated until serving.
3. In a separate bowl, beat cream until peaks form. Fold into sabayon (egg-champagne mixture) just before serving.

PRALINE WITH GINGER:

1 cup	sugar	250 mL
1 cup	almonds, skins on	250 mL
1 tablespoon	crystallized ginger (page 222)	15 mL

1. In a cast-iron skillet or sauté pan, combine sugar, almonds, and ginger over medium heat. Stirring constantly with wooden spoon, cook about 3 minutes, or until sugar melts and caramelizes, and almonds turn light brown.
2. Transfer mixture to a well-greased baking sheet and spread out evenly. Let cool. When mixture is crisp, crush coarsely with a rolling pin.

TO ASSEMBLE:

½ cup	maple walnut ice cream	125 mL
4	cooked fresh (above) OR canned peaches	4
1½ cups	champagne sabayon	375 mL
¼ cup	praline with ginger	50 mL

1. To assemble dessert, use 4 saucer-shaped champagne glasses. In each, place a 2-tablespoon (30-mL) scoop of maple walnut ice cream.
2. Cut cooked peaches in half and remove stones. Place 2 peach halves in each champagne glass.
3. Cover peaches with champagne sabayon.
4. Sprinkle each dish with 1 tablespoon (15 mL) praline-ginger. Serve at once.

SAUCES AND STOCKS

BÉARNAISE SAUCE

This is, for the most part, a tarragon-flavoured Hollandaise; we have substituted tarragon and vinegar for lemon juice. The sauce is great with grilled fish, grilled meats, broiled meats, and hamburger.
Yield: 1½ cups (375 mL).

1 tablespoon	finely chopped fresh tarragon OR 2 teaspoons (10 mL) dried	15 mL
1 tablespoon	finely chopped parsley OR chervil	15 mL
1 tablespoon	finely chopped shallots OR onion	15 mL
2 tablespoons	dry white wine	30 mL
¼ cup	red wine vinegar	50 mL
3	egg yolks	3
1 tablespoon	warm water	15 mL
½ cup	unsalted butter, melted	125 mL
½ teaspoon	freshly ground white pepper	2 mL
	Salt to taste	

1. In a saucepan over medium heat, combine ½ tablespoon tarragon, ½ tablespoon parsley, the shallots, wine, and wine vinegar. Cook, stirring, until liquid is reduced to half.
2. Strain, allow liquid to cool slightly, and pour into top of double boiler over simmering but not boiling water.
3. In a separate bowl, beat egg yolks with warm water. Slowly add egg mixture to double boiler, beating continuously.
4. Add melted butter in a slow, steady trickle, beating constantly. Sauce should have a velvety texture.
5. Remove sauce from heat. Season with pepper, salt, and remaining tarragon and parsley. Serve at once or store in sealed jar in refrigerator.

BÉCHAMEL SAUCE

To make any good sauce, use a heavy saucepan. It radiates heat evenly and keeps the roux - or flour mixture - from burning.

When making béchamel, be careful to use a hard flour. Do not use cake and pastry flour - your sauce will never thicken properly.

If you make more béchamel than you can use, freeze the unused portion in an ice-cube tray. To thaw, melt cubes in top of double boiler. Four cubes will equal about ½ cup (125 mL) sauce.

Yield: 2 cups (500 mL).

¼ cup	unsalted butter	50 mL
6 tablespoons	all-purpose flour	90 mL
2 cups	milk	500 mL
1	small onion, peeled, studded with 2 whole cloves	1
	Salt and freshly ground white pepper	
	Pinch of nutmeg	

1. Melt butter in a heavy saucepan over medium heat. Slowly add flour, stirring constantly for 2 minutes with wooden spoon. Be careful not to let flour burn or stick. Remove roux from heat and cool slightly.
2. Meanwhile, bring milk, with studded onion to boil in another saucepan. Remove from heat and very slowly add mix to roux, stirring constantly. Transfer onion to roux-milk mixture.
3. Season to taste with salt, white pepper, and nutmeg. Bring to boil. Reduce heat and simmer, uncovered, 20 minutes, stirring occasionally.
4. To serve, discard onion and strain sauce through fine sieve.

CRÈME FRAÎCHE

Crème fraîche, France's clotted cream, has the consistency of lightly whipped cream. It is excellent for thickening sauces and, because it has a slightly soured taste, complements sweet desserts and pies better than regular whipped cream.

Crème fraîche is extremely easy to make; in fact, it makes itself when left in a properly warmed environment–in a warm kitchen spot, on a stove over a pilot light, in front of a sunny window, or in a Styrofoam picnic cooler. It can be kept refrigerated, in sealed jars, for about 3 weeks.

Yield: 4 cups (1 L).

4 cups	heavy (35%) cream	1 L
1 tablespoon	buttermilk	15 mL

1. Pour 3 cups heavy cream into large screw-top jar. Add buttermilk; add last cup of cream. Gently shake jar to disperse buttermilk. Place lid on jar loosely.
2. Place jar in warm–about 70°F (21°C)–area free of drafts.
3. Let jar rest 14 to 18 hours. The timing will depend on freshness and make of cream, temperature, and so on. When cream has soured and stiffened, seal jar and refrigerate.

RASPBERRY SAUCE

This exceptionally memorable sauce may be made using either fresh or frozen raspberries.

Yield: 1¼ cups (300 mL).

¼ cup	sugar	50 mL
¼ cup	water	50 mL
1 cup	fresh OR frozen raspberries	250 mL
½ teaspoon	lemon juice	2 mL

1. In a saucepan, combine sugar and water and bring to boil, stirring until sugar is fully dissolved.
2. Add raspberries and lemon juice. Return to boil. Remove from heat, and force mixture through fine sieve before serving.

MUSHROOM SAUCE

This sauce is a natural for steaks, poultry, and hamburgers.
   Yield: 2 cups (500 mL), or enough sauce for 6 to 8 dinner entrées.

¾ pound	mushrooms	340 g
2 tablespoons	unsalted butter	30 mL
3 tablespoons	finely chopped onion	45 mL
1	clove garlic, finely chopped	1
½ teaspoon	freshly ground pepper	2 mL
½ teaspoon	finely chopped tarragon	2 mL
¼ teaspoon	thyme	1 mL
1 tablespoon	finely chopped parsley	15 mL
¼ cup	dry white wine	50 mL
2 cups	Brown Sauce (page 219)	500 mL
	Salt to taste	

1. Remove stems from mushrooms; trim and slice lengthwise into julienne sticks. Cut caps into slices ¼ inch (0.75 cm) thick.
2. Melt butter in a sauté pan over medium heat. When foam subsides, sauté onion until transparent.
3. Add mushrooms, garlic, and pepper and sauté 4 additional minutes, stirring continuously.
4. Add tarragon, thyme, and parsley. Stir. Increase heat to high, and add wine. Reduce liquid to half, stirring.
5. Reduce heat. Add Brown Sauce and simmer 5 minutes. Salt to taste.

HOLLANDAISE SAUCE

This is a classic French sauce of Dutch origin. Several tips may help you make a perfect egg-based sauce.

• Cook this sauce in a double boiler over hot, not boiling, water.

• Don't let your wrist relax. This sauce requires as much as 7 to 10 minutes of steady, continual beating. Don't take a break. A wire whisk works best.

• Always beat in one direction.

• If your egg sauce "breaks," or curdles, there are two techniques for restoring it. One: add a teaspoon or two of boiling water to the sauce and beat vigorously. The sauce should become smooth again. Two: place an egg yolk in a large bowl and very slowly add the curdled sauce to the new yolk. Pour very slowly, beating continuously with your whisk.

Yield: 1 cup.

3	egg yolks	3
1 tablespoon	water	15 mL
1 cup	butter, melted	250 mL
1 tablespoon	warm lemon juice	15 mL
¼ teaspoon	salt	1 mL
	Pinch of white pepper OR cayenne	

1. In top of a double boiler over simmering, but not boiling, water, combine egg yolks, water, and 1 teaspoon (5 mL) melted butter. Beat with whisk until smooth and creamy, about 7 minutes. Remove mixture from heat.
2. Continually beating mixure, add remaining butter in a very slow trickle. Beat until mixture thickens.
3. Add lemon juice, whisking thoroughly into sauce. Season with salt and pinch of white pepper or cayenne.
4. Serve or refrigerate in sealed jar for later use.

30-MINUTE BROWN SAUCE

Yield: 2 cups (500 mL).

2 tablespoons	unsalted butter	30 mL
1 cup	finely chopped onion	250 mL
1/2 cup	chopped celery	125 mL
1	carrot, sliced	1
1	bay leaf	1
1/2 teaspoon	black peppercorns	2 mL
1	clove garlic, crushed	1
1/2 teaspoon	thyme	2 mL
4	sprigs parsley	4
2 tablespoons	whole-wheat flour	30 mL
1/2 cup	dry red wine	125 mL
1 1/2 cups	canned beef consommé	375 mL
3 tablespoons	tomato paste OR pureé	45 mL
	Salt and freshly ground pepper	

1. Melt butter in a heavy saucepan over medium heat. Sauté onion, celery, carrot, bay leaf, peppercorns, garlic, thyme, and parsley until onion is browned.
2. Add flour, stirring constantly until flour browns.
3. Add wine, consommé, and tomato paste and bring to boil. Reduce heat and simmer, uncovered, 20 minutes. Salt and pepper to taste.
4. Strain sauce through fine sieve. Serve or refrigerate for later use.

MONTRÉAL MORNAY SAUCE

Many recipes for Mornay sauce call for two types of cheese – Parmesan and Gruyère. We have found the sauce just as tasty with all Parmesan.
Yield: 1 cup (250 mL).

1 cup	béchamel sauce (page 215)	250 mL
1 tablespoon	heavy (35%) cream	15 mL
¼ cup	grated Parmesan cheese	50 mL
	Pinch of cayenne	
1	egg yolk, lightly beaten	1
	Salt	

1. In a heavy saucepan, heat béchamel sauce over medium heat, stirring constantly with wooden spoon. When heated through, slowly add cream, Parmesan cheese, and cayenne. Continue to stir until cheese is fully melted and incorporated.
2. Reduce heat. Add yolk and stir. Keep sauce warm but do not boil. Salt to taste.

GREEN SAUCE

This is a tasty, colourful sauce for boiled fish, meat, vegetables, salads, and shrimp dishes. It goes well with Fredericton Fettuccine Salad (page 174) and is also a great dip.
Yield: 3 cups (750 mL).

2 tablespoons	finely chopped parsley	30 mL
1 tablespoon	finely chopped fresh OR 1½ teaspoons (7 mL) dried basil	15 mL
2	cloves garlic, finely chopped	2
5	anchovies, finely chopped	5
½ teaspoon	freshly ground pepper	2 mL
¼ teaspoon	salt	1 mL
½ teaspoon	ground cumin	2 mL
2½ cups	mayonnaise	625 mL

1. In a bowl, mix all ingredients thoroughly. Let sit at least 1 hour before serving. Refrigerate for later use.

SUPER SPAGHETTI SAUCE

There's nothing less pleasing than a spaghetti sauce made with unripened, flavourless tomatoes. In the height of summer, use Canada's ripe, bursting-at-the-seams tomatoes. The rest of the year, however, we suggest you adapt: substitute with canned tomatoes.

While this is called spaghetti sauce, don't be constrained by the spaghetti noodle; for fun, I give my kids almost any shaped noodle with this sauce—fusilli, elbow macaroni, or tagliatelle.

This sauce freezes well, so consider doubling or tripling the recipe. Seal the sauce in plastic containers, and store for future use.

Yield: 6 cups (1.5 L).

1 tablespoon	olive oil	15 mL
2	onions, finely chopped	2
1 pound	lean ground beef	450 g
2	cloves garlic, finely chopped	2
1	medium-sized carrot, thinly sliced	1
3 tablespoons	finely sliced celery	45 mL
10 cups	peeled, chopped tomatoes (about 5 pounds [2.2 kg] fresh OR 3 28-ounce [800-mL] cans, drained)	2.5 L
¼ cup	tomato paste	50 mL
1	bay leaf	1
1 teaspoon	oregano	5 mL
½ teaspoon	basil	2 mL
1 teaspoon	thyme	5 mL
2 tablespoons	ketchup	30 mL
1 tablespoon	salt	15 mL
½ teaspoon	freshly ground pepper	2 mL

1. In a saucepan, heat oil over medium heat. Add onion and sauté until transparent. Add ground beef and cook until beef begins to brown, stirring frequently to prevent burning.
2. Add garlic, carrot, and celery. Cook 3 to 4 minutes, stirring.
3. Add remaining ingredients. Bring to boil. Reduce heat and simmer, uncovered, 2½ hours. Serve or refrigerate.

CRYSTALLIZED GINGER

Ginger is one of the truly great spices of the world. Pungent, Eastern, and distinctive, the fresh root will keep for two weeks wrapped in plastic in the refrigerator.

In this book, we use a crystallized version of ginger. It will last for months stored in a cool place, even in the back of a cupboard. It adds a hint of ginger to many recipes, enhancing without overpowering.

Yield: enough for all the recipes in this book.

½ pound	fresh ginger root, peeled, cut into thin slices	225 g
1 pound	sugar, or enough to cover ginger	450 g

1. Sprinkle the bottom of a plastic container or a wide-mouthed glass jar with sugar.
2. Cover with layer of ginger slices. Cover with blanket of sugar. Cover with another layer of ginger slices and repeat, alternating with layers of sugar. Cover last ginger layer with thick blanket of sugar. Seal container and store in cool place for 1 month, or until ginger is crystallized.
3. Reserve the loose sugar as ginger layers are used for recipes that call for sugar and ginger as it will have absorbed some of ginger's flavour.

PEPPER SAUCE

Yield: 2 cups (500 mL).

2 teaspoons	unsalted butter	10 mL
1 tablespoon	very finely chopped onion	15 mL
1 teaspoon	coarsely crushed peppercorns	5 mL
½	bay leaf	½
½ cup	dry red wine	125 mL
1 tablespoon	brandy	15 mL
2 cups	Brown Sauce (page 219)	500 mL
3 tablespoons	heavy (35%) cream OR crème fraîche (page 216)	45 mL
	Salt	

1. Melt butter in a sauté pan over medium heat. When foam subsides, sauté onion about 1 minute.
2. Add crushed peppercorns and bay leaf and cook 1 additional minute.
3. Add wine and brandy and reduce liquid to half over high heat.
4. Reduce heat to medium. Add Brown Sauce and cook, stirring, 5 minutes. Add cream, bring sauce to boil, and remove from heat. Season to taste.

WAWA TARTAR

Like Wawa, Ontario, tartar has two identical halves. They liked it so much they named it twice.

Make our tartar sauce and we think you'll like it twice as much as any other version you've ever had.

Great with fish and seafood.

Yield: 2 cups (500 mL).

2 cups	mayonnaise	500 mL
3 tablespoons	finely chopped onion	45 mL
2 tablespoons	finely chopped parsley	30 mL
2 tablespoons	finely chopped dill	30 mL
3 tablespoons	finely chopped dill pickle	45 mL
1 tablespoon	capers, chopped	15 mL
2 teaspoons	lemon juice	10 mL
	Freshly ground pepper	

1. In a bowl, combine all ingredients and mix thoroughly. Refrigerate for later use.

INDEX